The Efficient Professional Series

The New Science of Time Management

**Why Emotional Awareness Matters Most
for Control of Your Schedule**

Robby Slaughter

Publisher
Method Press / An Imprint of AccelaWork
6100 Keystone #654
Indianapolis, IN 46220

For further information, please visit www.accelawork.com or
call 1-888-200-9387.

The New Science of Time Management

Cover design by AccelaWork
Photograph by jacoblund. Used with permission courtesy of
iStockPhoto.com.

July: 2019

For my beta readers:

(Who, in the spirit of efficiency,
provided their feedback simultaneously.)

Erin Aiello, Kevin Marshall, Zach Mielke,
Kathy Slaughter, Heather Sullivan,
Josh Wilson, and Nicole Wolfe.

Introduction: A New Science

WE'VE ALL SEEN WHAT HAPPENS with our time: it gets away from us. There are never enough hours in the day. We wake up with a million things to do, and we go to bed with a slightly different list of a million things to do.

The very idea of managing our time seems hopeless.

And yet, we live in a world of incredible innovation in science and technology. In each of our pockets is access to the sum of all human knowledge, instantly available with voice commands. We know more about how our species thinks, how our bodies work, and how we can engage with each other.

Despite these tremendous advancements, many of us feel as lost as ever. We are drowning in an overflow of information. Everyone wants our attention and our effort, but we can barely take care of our own needs.

So what's the answer?

It's not a cliché, and it's not easy. Like every generation before us, the secret to managing our time effectively is to swim with the current instead of against it.

We have to learn all about the new science and make it work for us.

Because all of us have the same 24 hours in a day, the same seven days in a week. The question is not the amount of time. It's not even what we *do* with the time.

It's something much more profound, and far more elusive: how we *feel* about what we have to do.

Because whether we like it or not, the emotional content of tasks is the greatest predictor of how they will affect us.

If we find them invigorating, we'll get lost. Hours will pass and feel like minutes. We'll cover tremendous ground in record time.

If we find them frustrating, every second will weigh on us like an endless annoyance.

That's why psychology is the best weapon we have. How often have you wanted to shut your brain off when it refused to do so, or get yourself thinking when you felt too foggy to operate? These are parts of our mental physiology which we know exist but can't seem to control.

But what if you knew how?

Using the latest in laboratory research, *The New Science of Time Management* tackles the problem with a fresh approach. Instead of purely focusing on time estimation and time blocking, these pages talk about how the brain actually works in our modern world.

Plus, the book includes activities for the reader to complete. Actually doing these is essential to success.

Because what really matters isn't just managing our time, it's understanding how we think about time, how we process our feelings about what lies ahead of us, and how we can be better stewards of the time we have.

That's what it means to manage time. It means being in control and knowing when we're not.

And that kind of awareness changes everything.

Are you ready?

About the Series

The Efficient Professional is a series of short, books that explain *precisely* how to increase your personal productivity at work.

There are many resources available filled with business advice. But unlike many others, The Efficient Professional offers exactly what steps you should take and provides hard evidence as to why.

Furthermore, this series focuses both on what to do as well as what *not* to do. Often, knowing what to avoid is even more important than knowing what to embrace.

Each book in the series contains a core idea that drives every recommendation. That means you don't need to memorize a vast number of rules or tips. Instead, the reader can build new habits around a single, easy-to-remember mission statement.

This way, referring back to different chapters and sections can be done quickly. Just recall the key concept, and turn to the needed page.

Finally, The Efficient Professional series offers fresh perspectives and does not merely rehash common sense. If you're ready to catapult your personal productivity, take a look at any book in the series.

More information at **efficientprofessional.com.**

About the Author

ROBBY SLAUGHTER is a workflow and productivity expert. His consulting practice assists a wide variety of organizations, including Fortune 500 companies, regional non-profits, small businesses and individual entrepreneurs to help increase productivity, simplify workflow and optimize business processes.

Robby's particular focus is the use of stakeholder-driven business improvement through the lens of processing mapping. Working with individuals and small teams, he facilitates discussions in which problems and opportunities are rapidly identified. The collaborative and visual nature of this approach has a substantial impact on organizations, who frequently see dramatic and sustained productivity gains within a few weeks.

Although this consulting process does not primarily employ technology, a background in computing drives their scientific approach to improvement. After an extensive career in IT systems development, Robby realized that the principal challenges affecting individual workers are not technological in nature, but psychological. He discovered that to become more effective and efficient at work, we need to empower individuals with authority and responsibility. His consulting practice now focuses exclusively on assessing workflow challenges, helping stakeholders to design and develop new business processes, and implement systematic, people-centered changes throughout the organization.

Robby is a frequent contributor to several regional and national magazines and has over one hundred published articles. He has been interviewed by several national and international publications, including the *Wall Street Journal*. Robby is a local and nationally known speaker. He is also the author of several books, including *Failure: The Secret to Success*, *The Unbeatable Recipe for Networking Events*, *The How-To Guide for Generations at Work*, *The Battle For Your Email Inbox*, and *The New Science of Time Management*. More information about Robby is online at robbyslaughter.com.

About this Book

THIS BOOK IS DIFFERENT than the others in *The Efficient Professional Series*, and different from many other books on the market. In recent years there have been tremendous advances in the science of psychology. Many of these ideas are just starting to trickle into the public consciousness. To aid the reader, this book features an appendix. When a key scientific finding is relevant to the text, it will be mentioned first as a full name followed by a short code. The abbreviation will appear when the phenomenon is referenced again. You can jump to the back of the book to learn more and then try to regain your place when you come back *[DWE]*, but you may be best served by using the appendix as a reference guide on subsequent readings.

Science is a fluid process by which new discoveries either strengthen or overturn old ideas. The study of the mind is an area which has undergone massive shifts in understanding in the last century. This is unlike mathematics (where geometry is largely unchanged since the days of the ancient Greeks) or physics (where Isaac Newton's equations are still taught in schools).

Psychology, however, is in the midst of a data-driven renaissance. Studies are now centered on rigorous statistical models and leverage the latest in neuroscience and brain imaging. A major effort is underway to reproduce the experiments of yesteryear to confirm they have the same results.

That means there's more to learn than you can reasonably cover in a four-year degree in the topic, and far more than can be effectively surveyed in a book. It also means that new discoveries appear on a daily basis that influence our understanding of effective time management.

Put these ideas to work in your own life. But, keep an eye on the news to see what comes next.

Your time is worth it.

Table of Contents

Chapter 1: Time Only Looks Like The Problem 19

Chapter 2: You Can't Manage Time, But You Can Predict It 27

Chapter 3: The Best and Worst Part of Our Lives: Other People 35

Chapter 4: The Energy of Activity..45

Chapter 5: The Unstoppable Power of Results...............................55

Chapter 6: Inside the Task Sorting Machine................................65

Chapter 7: Outside the Task Sorting Machine 79

Chapter 8: Operating the Machine...89

Chapter 9: Do's and Don'ts of Time Management 107

Chapter 10: The Administrative Assistant 121

Chapter 11: The Overbearing Boss..133

Chapter 12: The Exhausted Account Manager 145

Chapter 13: The Distracted Entreprenuer 153

Chapter 14: A Review of Everything.....................................163

Appendix: A Basis in Science..173

Chapter 1

Time Only Looks
Like the Problem

"Time is what we want most, but what we spend worst."
–William Penn

LET'S FACE IT: You can't really manage your time. We use the phrase "time management" often, but those words imply that time can be "managed." *[ICO]* They tell us time can be moved around, adjusted, and prodded. That we can stretch it or shrink it. That we can shuffle the available hours like cards in our hand and play them out in the order we think is best.

But time is not like this. We say time is a "resource" but it's not like capital or inventory. *[ICR]* You can't store time in a vault and use it later. You can't loan time to a friend or borrow it from a bank. You can't use your time quickly or slowly. In fact, all you can do is spend it second by second. *[FR]*

And if you're unhappy with how you passed the time, you can't demand a refund.

Yet, this is the topic of countless books, seminars, videos, and pamphlets on time management. We think we can manage time, but really all we can do is *experience* time. What we can manage is what we do with our time, but even that can be challenging.

Perhaps the biggest limitation on our time is **interruptions**. This is anything that happens which draws away our focus. Interruptions are often people who come into our view or insert themselves into our attention span. They tap on our shoulders, and they come into our workspace. They shout over the cubicle walls or flag us down. They call us, text us, tweet at us, message us, or email us. They think we're thinking what *they* are thinking. [FCE]

And what's worse, they use the most innocuous of phrases: "Got a minute?"

Of course, interruptions are also caused by systems. Alarm clocks interrupt our rest. Schoolhouse buzzers interrupt our classrooms. Intercoms interrupt our concentration. And in many places there are honking horns, ringing phones, whirring machines, and blinking lights. It's amazing that we can get any work done at work anymore.

Plus, the urgency communicated by these interruptions is often wildly inflated. Someone who pokes their head in your office for a "quick question" probably doesn't actually need an answer right then. It's likely that incoming phone call could responsibly be sent to voicemail. And the ding of that email message might make it seem like you need to read it right away. But if that was the case, why would they have sent an email?

The innumerable list of interruptions are only matched by the huge variety of **distractions** in our modern world. Unlike an interruption—which comes from other people—distractions are entirely caused by a lack of discipline.

While you're reading this book, there's plenty to be distracted by. The pain in your hip. The creak in the chair.

Those papers on your desk you've been meaning to organize. A project in your garage, or an unanswered email.

Or, you might be distracted by thoughts of your next vacation *[DG]* or fond memories of your last one. *[RHE]* Distractions can be incomplete work, fantasies of leisure, or anything in between.

Plus, there's not much you can do besides attempt to concentrate. You can try sealing yourself off in a featureless room with no windows and no wifi, but this will make it impossible for others to reach you. We need to be able to be interrupted. And we need to be *able* to be distracted too: that's the primary source of creativity. *[CF]*

Discipline is essential. But, so is knowing when to be undisciplined. *[IE]*

That decision-making process illustrates another reason why it's so hard to manage time: **inaccuracy**. Like the novice playing darts, when we try to estimate how much time something will take we are all over the place. *[DKE] [KETE]*

And usually, we tend to be wrong. If we are too conservative, it's because we're afraid of missing the deadline, getting in trouble, or other people screwing up. So, we pad the schedule.

Or, we're too aggressive. We are afraid we'll appear lazy, or we're trying to impress someone. *[SDB]* Or, we don't want to be accused of padding the schedule. And we run behind.

Accuracy isn't the only problem. We're also imprecise when we budget our time.

What's the difference? Accuracy is being centered around the target, but precision is being consistent in our aim.

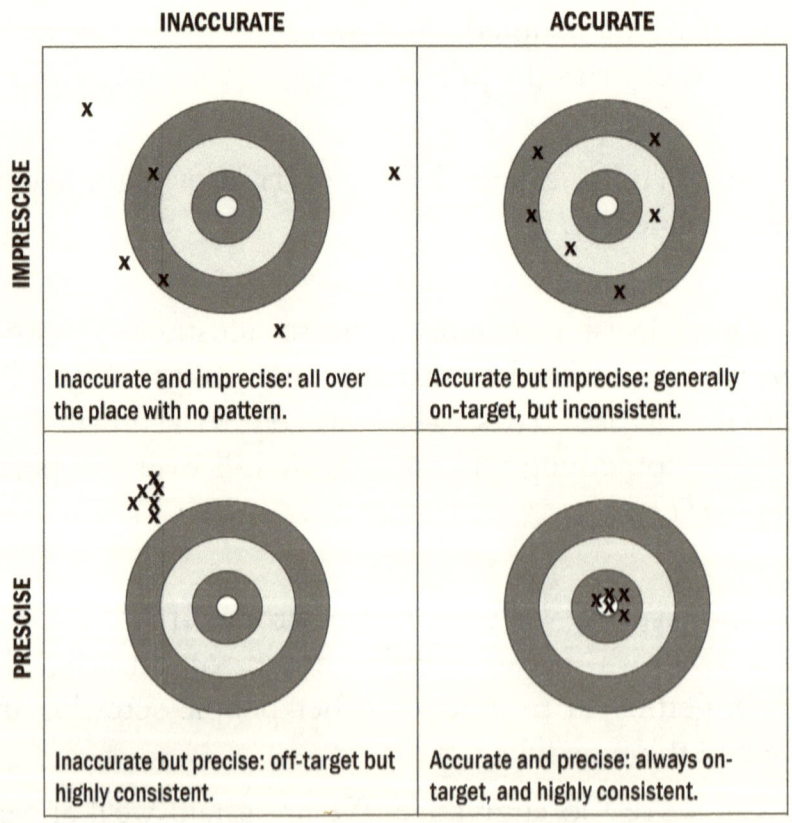

	INACCURATE	ACCURATE
IMPRECISE	Inaccurate and imprecise: all over the place with no pattern.	Accurate but imprecise: generally on-target, but inconsistent.
PRECISE	Inaccurate but precise: off-target but highly consistent.	Accurate and precise: always on-target, and highly consistent.

Generally speaking, people are bad at time estimation. *[KETE]* One reason we lack accuracy is because we make appraisals in weeks and months instead of hours and minutes. In the classic book on software project planning *The Mythical Man Month*, author Fred Brooks argues that you cannot estimate work in a coarse unit of measure. Instead, we need to imagine shorter intervals and smaller tasks. And if we're unwilling to break down a unit of work into smaller pieces *[GST]*, that means we don't really know how to do it.

In a sense, we're standing too far from the target to hit the target all that well.

And as for precision, that mostly comes from experience. To get better at estimating consistently, we need to do it more often. That requires reflecting on past projects as well as being intentional about making plans for the future.

Not knowing how to do something is about self-awareness, and awareness is fundamentally about respect. If we think highly of ourselves and others, we *should* know our capacities and limitations and speak honestly about them. *[DKE]* But often, the opposite is the case: we *believe* we are experts but in the end aren't able to deliver in the way that is needed. *[EDG]* And sometimes, a lack of respect is the key reason why time management is so hard.

A common refrain is to "jealously guard your time." That phrase, however, encourages everyone to be on the defensive. Are people coming into your space, trying to steal your time? If everyone adopts this posture, tensions will run high *[EC]* and no one can collaborate.

All of us share the same second, every second, so all of our time is equally important. But when someone asks us to drop what we are doing to help them, they may be disrespecting our right to focus. And when we leap to be helpful, we may be disrespecting ourselves.

Plus, a huge part of respecting and disrespecting time is the hierarchy we create in the world. Some people won't answer a call if they don't know the number. Some people have administrative assistants that act as "gatekeepers." Those who consider themselves more important and more powerful assign tasks to others which would be a "waste of their time" to tackle personally.

Yet, don't we all want to be known as the helpful person who volunteers? *[BWE]*

And ultimately, isn't the use and abuse of others' time is a conduit for resentment?

You cannot manage time any more than you can control other people, but you can **manage your own reactions.** In fact, learning to take the reins over how we react to other people's bids for our time is the essential challenge.

It's the one that's most often overlooked. And it's also the aspect of time management which has the most potential to transform our lives.

Chapter 2

You Can't Manage Time, But You Can Predict It

"Energy, not time, is the fundamental currency of high performance." —Jim Loehr

YOU CANNOT MANAGE TIME. Like a mighty river, it will flow endlessly. Once you are in the waters, you will be carried along with the current.

But you *can* manage your energy. You can decide how to react to events in the world around you and make choices that impact how you feel.

Take a simple example. Imagine a piece of chocolate (or your favorite treat.) Close your eyes and contemplate how it feels to unwrap it. Listen inside the echo chamber of your mind to the crinkle of the foil. Remember how it smells. Now, place the virtual candy into your mouth and enjoy that distinct, memorable flavor and texture. Swallow, and smile.

If you really take a moment to do this exercise—and you are honest with yourself—you'll find you do feel a tiny bit better and more relaxed afterward. You might feel a little bit more motivated to do some work. Even though you were only *imagining* that small pleasure, your mind helped create some of the effect as if you had it for real. *[CC]*

And if just *thinking* about a bit of sugar can do that, consider what would happen if you actively managed your emotions. **If you were conscious of your emotions and how they impacted you, what would that do to your time management?**

This concept is called *emotional energy*. In recent years, the word "energy" has taken on new meanings. In classical physics and the hard sciences, energy is a property of objects that can be transferred to other objects, but in a closed system is neither created or destroyed. A charged battery has energy. A full water tower has energy. A rolling ball has energy. All of these forms of energy can be calculated, measured, and put to practical use.

The same term is used in philosophy, metaphysics, and spirituality. In traditional Chinese culture, *qi* (also written as *ch'i*), is thought of as an active life force that surrounds living things and gives them strength and purpose. In some Indian religions, a *chakra* is believed to be an energy point within a spiritual body. The word *aura* is also used to describe a luminous, yet invisible energy field radiating off of a person. While all of these ideas may have personal significance to some individuals, they cannot be measured and put to practical use in the same manner as the scientific concept of energy.

Researchers working in the positive psychology movement, however, have a third definition of energy which bridges the gap between how we feel and what we can measure and use in engineering and technology. They explain:

> Emotional energy is a type of positive affective arousal, which people can experience as emotion—short responses to specific events—or mood—longer-lasting affective states that need not be a response to a specific event.

That quote comes from an article titled "Energy Management of People in Organizations: A Review and Research Agenda" from the *Journal of Business and Psychology*. But since it's written in dry academic language, let's break down those first few words:

1.   **Positive:** We're only really concerned with impacts that are uplifting, exciting, or encouraging.

2.   **Affective:** One of the ABC's of modern psychology. Instead of b for behavior (how life history and patterns are reflected in everyday actions) and c for cognition (how we think, evaluate options, and make purposeful decisions), affect is the *immediate* experience of feeling an emotion.

3.   **Arousal:** This word describes going from a state of being apathetic to one of being interested. Our pulse quickens, our eyes widen, and our breath gets a little shorter.

To think of it this way: **emotional energy is the sensation of engagement**. It comes about sometimes as emotions in response to a single event, or sometimes as a mood related to our own life rhythms. *[CT]*

On a personal level, you've experienced this. A kind word from a friend can help you feel better about yourself and want to get back to work. *[PRI]* And you've had days—although certainly not enough of them—in which you feel like you're on fire. You're knocking things out left and right, you're highly productive, and you feel like the king or queen of your domain. *[FL]* These experiences are the pinnacle of emotional energy.

The goal of this book is this: **teach you to make them happen on purpose so you can maximize the use of your time.**

Because what is science for if it doesn't make our lives better?

To help you build a stronger understanding of the curious nature of emotional energy, think about the tasks you have to do all the time. Some of these things you love doing, and some you can't stand. In a few cases we tend to have these in common. Most people enjoy cleaning themselves. A hot shower or a relaxing bath is typically a pleasant part of the day. But most people don't enjoy cleaning their homes—especially if someone else contributed to the mess. *[OC]*

Likewise, there are probably activities at work you dread and activities you can't wait to complete. For most people, getting through meetings and emails falls squarely in the first category. And for many, a good brainstorming session, a deadline that's been met, or a customer testimonial fits into the second. But we're all different and knowing what will trigger our own emotional energy is absolutely essential to improving our time management skills.

In its simplest form, emotional energy management is recommended by the Brian Tracy book *Eat That Frog!* As the old expression suggests, if you are required to do something as disgusting as swallowing a live amphibian every day, probably the best course of action is to do it first and get it over with. That way you won't be dreading it for hours until it's done. *[RBE]*

But this advice alone isn't nearly enough to understand emotional energy. Consider the following:

- There are likely people in your life who **energize** you, that you can't wait to see and who will help you feel empowered for the rest of the day.

- There are likely people in your life who **drain** you. You don't look forward to meeting with them, you know they are going to weigh you down with work or emotional baggage, and they may deaden your motivation after they leave.

- There are probably **bits of work that you love** and **bits of work you hate**, and these items aren't always even consistent. *[SCT]*

- You likely have **good days** and **bad days**, good weeks and bad weeks. And sometimes you don't even know why.

So what's the solution? It's more than eating a frog. It's more than trying to make yourself focus. It's more than running from problems and running toward the weekend.

Instead the answer is all about **prediction**. You must know yourself in order to improve yourself. We are all affected by emotional energy in different ways, but we are all impacted.

The solution is best known as a mantra. Read it. Memorize it. Write it on a sticky note and put it on your mirror.

> **Predict your emotional energy to optimize your professional experience.**

In other words, first try to imagine how you will feel based on what you have to do. Then, decide what to do in order to feel best.

Uncovering this information is like finding money when doing laundry. You didn't know it was there, and it may influence your thinking more than you might anticipate. *[EE]*

Because what we usually do is merely make a rapid decision about what we will do next and then feel like we made the best choice. *[CB]* But over the long run, are we productive? Are we satisfied? Do we feel in control of our time and our outcomes?

The way to track progress is of course using lists and calendars. But the magic is in making the predictions.

That's the secret. That's the answer. But to find out how to do it, turn the page.

Chapter 3

The Best and Worst Part of Our Lives: Other People

"How people treat other people is a direct reflection of how they feel about themselves." —Paulo Coelho

IN THE LAST FEW YEARS, two words have become part of the everyday language of business. *Introverts* are people who tend to revert back to being alone and undisturbed to recharge. *Extroverts*, on the other hand, prefer to spend time with people and use high-energy relationships to reset and motivate themselves.

You probably have already put yourself into one of these categories. You may feel that most of the time you'd rather be left alone, or most of the time you want to be at a party telling stories and making people laugh. Maybe you tend to hover on the line between the two extremes. Or perhaps you find yourself introverted in some situations and extroverted in others.

It's important to know yourself, but to use emotional energy to maximize your time management skills you must understand how you relate to other people. *[IBIT]* Knowing our differences from others—as well as the variations in mood and situation—forms the basis for better relationships and better time management.

Think of the last person who you met with for a meeting. It could be your boss for your annual review. Or, an informal conversation with your coworker at your desk. It might be a sales call or a vendor, or even a phone call. Now, answer these seven questions about that meeting:

1. Is this a person who tends to give me energy or take my energy away? That is, do I feel *more* excited after meeting them, drained, or no change at all? *[PP]*

2. Do I feel different when I am merely in the same room with this person or do I need to have an actual conversation with them to feel different? *[SVT]*

3. If this person said "I've been thinking about you" would that make me feel appreciated or fill me with dread, or something else? *[BFE]*

4. Is this person generally one who takes work off my plate or gives me more work to do?

5. Am I happy they do that with my work? Do they take away stuff I don't like or give me stuff I *do* like, or vice versa?

6. Is this the kind of person who often has a gift for me or who expects me to get them a gift (or do them a favor)?

7. Do I feel this person respects my time?

Repeat the exercise again a few times but think of other people in your life. Try closing your eyes as you reflect on each question. *[IBE]* Select individuals who have a different relationship with you and a different personality each time.

Every person is unique. And furthermore, every *situation* is distinct. If you're in a good mood and they are in a bad one that is probably not going to be the same experience for each of you.

It's possible to change the people in your life, but it's not easy. You can get a new job with new coworkers. You can move to a new area of town and get new neighbors. You can stop returning calls from one set of friends and start making new ones. But usually you're going to end up with a mix of people, and not all of those interactions will go beautifully every time—no matter how much we think it's up to us. [OC]

Let's take a common situation that impacts our ability to manage time: meetings. Suppose you've got an appointment on your calendar to meet Sue Smith at 9:00am next Tuesday. Consider the following system:

BEFORE—Add a second appointment on your calendar just for yourself to prepare for the meeting with Sue. Make it as long as you think you need to get ready: 15 minutes, a half hour, or more. Here are some questions to ask:

Q: If the amount of time you need to prepare is negligible, are you sure you should even have the meeting?

Q: If you don't feel the need to prepare or don't want to go, can you turn this meeting into a phone call or an email?

Q: Are you sure the meeting is at the right time, given your personality [CT] and your work the rest of your work for the day?

DURING—Ensure the meeting is actually on your calendar, even if you know when it's going to be. *[ZE]* Ask the person how long you need for the conversation and make your calendar appointment the same length. Consider these questions:

Q: Do you believe the proposed start time is when the meeting will start? If not, be ready to do something else in case they are late.

Q: Do you believe the proposed end time is when the meeting will end? If not, add buffer time in your schedule, or announce a hard deadline so you can leave on time.

Q: Do you have questions you want to ask or information you want to share at the meeting? If so, can you relay them in advance via email, maybe even get some answers? And if not, does this meeting even need to happen?

Q: Do you know what questions you might be asked? If so, can you write a report in advance? If not, can you solicit questions via email, and possibly eliminate the need for the meeting entirely?

AFTER—If you predict that you'll have to do some work immediately afterward or you know you'll feel drained by this meeting, block that out on your calendar. Consider these questions at that time:

Q: Do you predict you will feel more: appreciated, anxious, or angry?

Q: Did your workload change due to this meeting? If it increased, add it to your calendar or task list. If it decreased, add something else that is next in importance.

Q: Is there a part of this meeting you need to remember, or did you learn a lesson for your next meeting with this person? Write it down or tell someone else about it. *[RHE]*

When you combine all of these ideas together along with everything else on your calendar, the way you structure your time may change.

Instead of merely reserving blocks for particular activities, you will begin to think about what leads up to those activities and follows them. You'll reserve space to prepare and to recover. You'll set aside time for travel. And you may realize that you really have quite a bit more to do than you than you planned.

Take a look at what your calendar might look before and after applying these concepts:

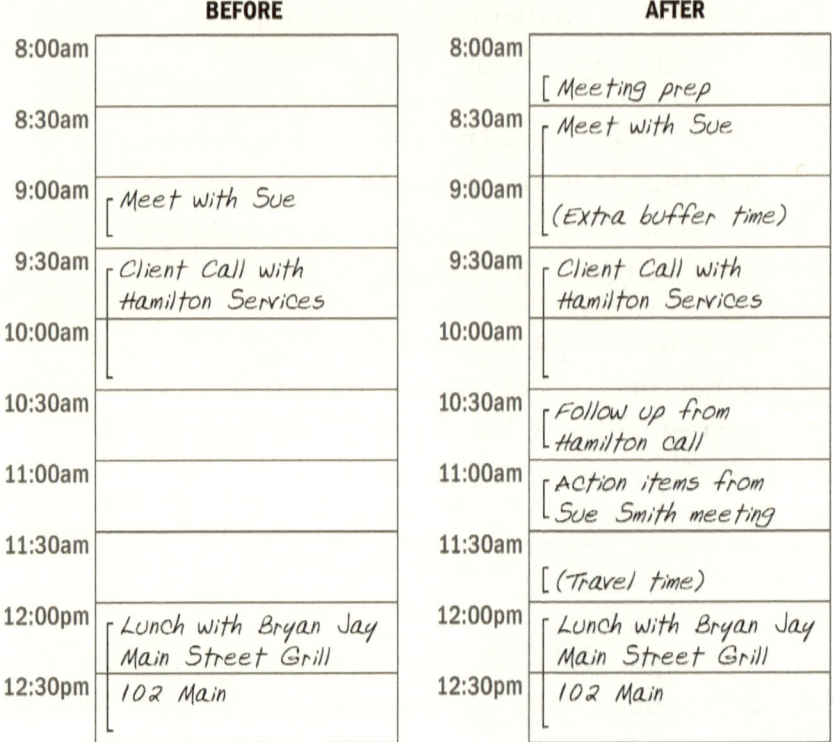

BEFORE		AFTER	
8:00am		8:00am	
			[Meeting prep
8:30am		8:30am	⌐ Meet with Sue
9:00am	⌐ Meet with Sue	9:00am	
	⌊		(Extra buffer time)
9:30am	⌐ Client Call with Hamilton Services	9:30am	⌐ Client Call with Hamilton Services
10:00am	⌊	10:00am	⌊
10:30am		10:30am	⌐ Follow up from ⌊ Hamilton call
11:00am		11:00am	⌐ Action items from ⌊ Sue Smith meeting
11:30am		11:30am	[(Travel) time)
12:00pm	⌐ Lunch with Bryan Jay Main Street Grill	12:00pm	⌐ Lunch with Bryan Jay Main Street Grill
12:30pm	102 Main ⌊	12:30pm	102 Main ⌊

There's more on the calendar now, but less uncertainty. Sudden scrambles are less likely, and the impact of the meeting is more apparent.

Just rearranging your schedule is only the first step. There's far more you can do to better understand other people. It is these individuals, after all, who will impact your ability to manage your time the most. [SDB]

You can take personality tests, or you can ask them to do so. You can use the classic Myers-Briggs instrument, the DiSC profile, or the scientifically-supported Five Factor Model. [PTT] You can ask them how they prefer to communicate, or how you prefer to communicate with them.

But in the end, every person you know and every interaction you have with them is likely to make you feel one of three ways: **appreciated**, **anxious**, or **angry**.

And why does this matter? Because of the core concept of taking control of your time:

> **Predict your emotional energy to optimize your professional experience.**

Once you understand how people tend to make you feel, you can often predict how they might make you feel in the future.

And once you can look ahead to the future with even a tiny degree of confidence, you can begin to plan better. *[OC]*

You can decide how to prepare to meet with people, what to do in the meeting, and even be ready for what you'll be doing afterward. And sometimes, you'll be able to skip the meeting altogether.

Once you start to better manage your own expectations around other people, it's time to turn toward yourself.

But not your personality: **your task list.**

That's why we need to shift from managing emotional energy solely with respect to people toward managing emotional energy with respect to activity.

Take a deep breath, and let's get started.

Chapter 4

The Energy of Activity

"All growth depends upon activity. There is no development physically or intellectually without effort, and effort means work." –Calvin Coolidge

GO FIND A COMPLETELY BLANK SHEET OF PAPER. Not a sticky note. Not the back of an envelope. Get a full-sized sheet of printer or copy paper, and a pen.

Now, put this book down and write down everything you have to do at this moment. Make a big list of all of the current action items, large and small, that you need to be working on. Include absolutely everything weighing on your mind, from the laundry to an unreturned text message. This book will be here when you return.

If you really committed yourself to that project, that piece of paper is likely filled front and back. It has stuff you need to buy at the grocery store. It includes voicemails you've listened to and emails you've read but where your responses are still forthcoming. That list has unpaid debts and almost-broken promises. There are dreams and goals of enormous magnitude, and there are middling, tiny tasks that you know you could have done in the time it took to read this paragraph. It's an inventory of everything to do.

The danger in this activity is that sometimes crease a false sense of accomplishment. [MOL] The list can be useful, but it's the work that matters.

If you've ever worked in retail, in a warehouse, or in another setting where you are managing physical goods, the term *inventory* may send shivers down your spine. The inventory is where the money is. The company has most of its capital tied up in whatever is sitting in the shelves, waiting to be sold. And on regular intervals, you are required to "do inventory," which means to check the list of what you *think* you have against what is *actually* there.

The record of what exists is as important as the items themselves. Without an accounting of every product you have for sale, you can't really know how the business is doing. And in much the same way a business owner gets a little rush from taking something down and making a sale to a customer, we often feel a burst of energy when we cross something off our list. *[CC]*

This is energy of activity. It's feeling good because we just did something. And while you may be totally exhausted by the enormous list you just created, here's one more thing to do.

Find something quick on that list that you can do right now and do it. Go. Don't come back here until you're done.

If you completed that task, you are probably experiencing one of two emotions. If you're glad it's done, you've got a sense of **relief**. Finally, that one is checked off your list. You've been meaning to get to it, and now you've done it. Congratulations! *[OC]*

But in some cases, completing a task can bring about a sense of **regret**. It was something you needed to do, but you don't feel all that much better after the fact. *[IE]* Sometimes just because something is done doesn't mean it's over. It may stay with you despite the task being completed.

Here are some examples of tasks that may lead to relief or regret:

Relief	Regret
Getting your phone bill paid on time	Making a child support payment
Submitting a job application	Laying off a valuable employee
Turning in a final report	Calling a customer to apologize for an error
Getting the laundry folded and put away	Donating clothing that doesn't fit because you gained weight
Making it to the post office before they close	Throwing out expired ingredients for a favorite recipe

Sometimes you might feel *both* relief and regret but pay more attention to whether or not you wish you never had to do the task in the first place. After all, it might be satisfying to finally follow up with that contact you've been meaning to get to for a while, but not so much if you also feel terrible for how long you've put it off. *[RBE]*

And furthermore, it might be the case that a task is part of a much larger project. You might have a sense of relief about the individual task, but regret about the state of the overall endeavor.

Why is this important? Because human beings are driven by emotional energy. When we are relieved, we often get a burst of excitement that leads to the next task. When we feel regret, we may have a sensation of sadness that will leads us to a glass of wine.

When you look at your task list, you can likely predict how you'll feel when each task is done. Keep these words in mind: **relief (r)** or **regret (R)**. And then, consider every other way you might like to categorize your tasks.

Whether something will produce a sense of elation or frustration isn't always easy to recognize. But many other aspects of our work are more obvious. Some things we **desire** to do and others we **dislike**. And of course if we're not careful, we will only do the fun stuff. We'll put off what we don't enjoy for as long as we can, and we may skip it entirely. *[IC]*

Likewise, most of us don't live in the middle of the woods with no other people around. We can delegate tasks to others. We can have the kids do chores (although supervision may be required), and we can ask our colleagues to pitch in on key projects.

With the rise of the Internet, there are more opportunities than ever to hand off tasks to somebody else. Whether you need someone to transcribe audio, edit a document, run an errand, give you a ride, do some research, write software, complete a data entry project, or almost anything else you can think of, there are places online to make that happen.

But there are some tasks it just seems like you have to do yourself. *[OC]* Some work has to be **owned** by you; some work can be **outsourced**. We can usually tell the difference right away. But we rarely ask for help.

Why is that? Perhaps the most obvious reason is it's stressful to delegate work. The old expression says: "If you want something done right, you have to do it yourself."

It often seems like no one will work as hard as we will. *[SCL]* That's not always true, of course. The entire story of humanity is people working together because some tasks were handed off to other people. But it can be stressful to outsource work, especially when you can't supervise it personally.

There's another factor in retaining ownership over tasks. That's when we feel like we're the only one who can do the work: that it requires a unique set of **skills** that only we have. Or, perhaps we think the work doesn't need any special knowledge or ability. In that case, the task seems **simple**. Why bother to give it to someone else when we can just do it immediately? *[EDG]*

And sometimes, the difficulty of a project is part of its allure. Maybe we want to do something that is **challenging**. That's why people spend hours with a book of sudoku or crossword puzzles, or playing video games that are effectively huge logic puzzles. But challenging doesn't always mean that it's stimulating. Going for a run requires discipline, and you have to keep reminding yourself to maintain your best possible speed. For most of us, exercise is a challenge.

And other times, it's nice to do something which is **casual**. This might be as straightforward as vacuuming or something that once you learn to do doesn't require much attention, like knitting. Tasks might require intense focus or be so routine that you impress someone watching but can easily carry on a conversation. Each could be important, but they are different.

This gives us five areas in total, with each requiring either low or high energy:

Low Energy	High Energy
Relief (r)	Regret (R)
Desire (d)	Dislike (D)
Owned (o)	Outsourced (O)
Simple (s)	Skillful (S)
Casual (c)	Challenging (C)

For everything on our plate, it may leave us with a feeling of **relief** or **regret**. For every task we have to tackle, we might have the **desire** to complete it or the **dislike** that it even exists. It could be something we alone must **own**, or that we can **outsource** to someone else. The work is often so **simple** that even a novice could do it, but other times it requires a high level of **skill**. And it may be a **casual** task that requires almost no brain power, or a **challenging** task that takes our complete focus.

Answering these questions help to understand the energy of activity. It's why we avoid some entire sections of our list and leap headfirst into others. It's why we end up drained by a few select items and rejuvenated by others. And it's why merely *reading* the list often causes us to experience the feelings we anticipated. *[SFP]*

Understanding the energy of activity gives us the ability to better prioritize. Remember that if we know what's going to happen, we can better adjust. That's the key concept of this book:

> **Predict your emotional energy to optimize your professional experience.**

So get your priorities under control. Decide what to do first, second, third, and last.

And the reason we need to put work in the right order? That's easy.

It's because results are what we want.

Chapter 5

The Unstoppable Power of Results

"To conquer frustration, one must remain intensely
focused on the outcome, not the obstacles." –T.F. Hodge

THE AMERICAN PHILOSOPHER WILLIAM JAMES once wrote that "Nothing is so fatiguing as the eternal hanging on of an uncompleted task."

That's a comment about the overwhelming stress of modern life: always having things to do and never having enough time to do to them. But feeling like we can't keep up is nothing new. William James penned that line in 1886.

Almost all of us love checking things off our list. *[ZE]* Getting it done, knocking it out, crossing it off, or marking it "finished." There is an intense satisfaction in completing a goal, even if it's a small one. And what's more, tiny victories often take less time than we might have imagined and have a greater emotional impact than we would have predicted.

Try it yourself: if you're at home, look around. Are there dishes to be done, trash to be taken out, or laundry to be folded?

If you're in a public place, can you organize what's on your person, clear out voicemails or text messages from your phone, or check your calendar to see what is next?

Put this book down and take note of the time that passes while you complete that minuscule project. When you return, analyze how you feel. Was it worth the handful of seconds it took? Don't you feel a tiny bit better for having finished what needed to be done?

We are often energized by results. Sometimes, how we *think* we're going to feel once we're past that post can be a source of motivation. But other times, getting it done isn't a relief.

There's a difference between the emotions associated with *doing* an activity and those associated with *having done* that activity. **In short: sometimes we like what we get but not what we have to do.**

Understanding the distinction between activity and results may seem self-evident, but it's how we structure our time and our work. *[SCT]* For example, we tend to pay people by the hour, not by the project. We usually write instructions rather than requirements. But often we don't want to actually be the person completing the task. Rather, we want the task to be completed.

Knowing which we want is key to managing our time better. Recall the guiding principle:

> **Predict your emotional energy to optimize your professional experience.**

So ask yourself: do I personally want to do the work, or do I just want the work done?

In order to understand our relationship with results, one of the best places to look is into our past. What have you already done (or failed to do) and how has it impacted you? What emotions are you managing about your past victories and defeats? And in addition to how reflecting on those may impact your mood, these past experiences can influence your confidence.

Grab a piece of paper and start with today. What have you already accomplished after getting up? Make a list of anything you've done since you rolled out of bed—but only include items that you *don't* do every day.

Go ahead. Try it now.

You've just produced the opposite of a to-do list. Instead of being about the future, it's about the past. This is a just-did list. Or maybe, a "results list." It features not what you want, but what you already accomplished.

There's also scientific evidence of a positive impact from adding reflection to your daily routine. *[GE]* This could be a gratitude journal or an accomplishment tracker. Some people like to channel their childhood with stickers and gold stars. Try something that works for you.

But the idea of reviewing our results doesn't just have to be completed day-by-day. You can do it each week, each month, and each year of your life. What else have you accomplished? Were you once accepted into a prestigious organization? Did you graduate from high school, college, or finish a certificate program? Did you run a 5K or get over your fear of skydiving? Were you given an award? Did you slog your way through a difficult book? There is significance in taking stock of what you've done.

However, victories might not always be triumphant. Maybe you got out of a bad relationship. Maybe you learned how to live with a disease. Perhaps you moved on from a dark chapter in your life. Sometimes the accomplishment is about successfully letting go.

Whatever you did, it helped bring you here today. And the psychology of results gives us a sense of drive that has incredible power.

So now that you finished your just-did list, grab a new sheet of paper. On this, write out what results you have achieved in life that give you meaning.

Don't be afraid to put anything down as long as it's meaningful to you. It might include impressing one teacher, singing one karaoke song in front of strangers, or cooking one meal that came out amazing.

Write your life-done list. Fill the whole page. And then, come back.

Now that you're feeling empowered, it's time to discuss ways to use the unstoppable power of results to better plan your life.

There are three key methods to doing this. First, **plan** to get something done every day. Second, **outsource** activities, but retain ownership over results. And finally, **break large wins into small wins** for extra momentum.

This first piece of advice to plan to get something done every day is deceptively simple. Of course we want to have accomplishments on a daily basis. What would be the point of going to work or getting up in the morning if we weren't going to knock something off our list?

The reason this is difficult is because we frequently forget to take credit for what we've completed. If it wasn't planned, we don't acknowledge it.

That's why starting the day by listing no more than three things that you know you can do is always worth doing. These can be as routine as making the bed or as unique as placing a call you've been meaning to make.

Write them down. Check them off. Get the energy of results—and keep going.

Next up: delegation. We know we can't do everything, and one of the best ways to leverage our time is to leverage our relationships.

You can outsource tasks. And in this modern era, you can use the Internet or your smartphone to find someone to give you a ride, clean your house, edit a document, take some photographs, research products, or anything else you need to do.

Of course, asking someone else to handle it for you has its downsides. There is often a cost, and you may not get the quality you'd get if you did the work yourself.

But the larger problem is often the emotional impact. If we delegate, we may be anxious until the task is complete. And unlike a personal accomplishment, we don't have the automatic satisfaction of having done well at something we chose to do.

That's why it's crucial to retain ownership over results, even if we offload the work to someone else. This starts with the to-do list item itself. Instead of writing "return library books" put "ensure library books are returned." *[EE]* This small twist in language leads to a big twist in emotion. *[FR]* We feel more like managers of our own affairs rather than helplessly rushing from one task to the next.

Delegate, but still be in charge. You'll feel more accomplished because you made sure the work got done.

The final technique for making results part of taking control of your time is this: **break large wins into small wins for extra momentum.**

This sounds like the age-old advice about how to eat a whole elephant. You do it one bite at a time.

But the difference is to do something smarter than simple subdivision of goals into projects, projects into activities, and activities into tasks. Instead, take the overall result that you desire and convert that into individual pieces that also feel satisfying. *[SFP]*

Trying to get a new job? Make a goal to apply for four positions in one day, and celebrate after each one.

Hoping to get a promotion at work? Design a plan consisting of a portfolio, a new professional outfit, and identifying and meeting with a new mentor. Each big step deserves its own moment of self-approval.

Big results feel amazing. But they still feel great if they are celebrated in stages as well as at the end.

Break it down and knock it out of the park.

A turn-of-the-century expression quips "those who say it cannot be done are always being interrupted by those who are doing it."

Results have unstoppable power. No matter how down we feel or how skeptical we might be, those who are making things happen have an undeniable momentum.

That's why we must focus on the psychology of accomplishment. Along with the energy of activity and the relationships (and perceptions) we have of others *[SVT]*, these are the three keys to gaining control over our time.

It's with this understanding that we can become radically more productive and more satisfied.

It's with this mentality that our lives can be both relaxing and engaging.

You have the theory. Now, it's time to put it into practice.

Onward!

Chapter 6

Inside the Task Sorting Machine

"Planning is bringing the future into the present so that you can do something about it now." –Alan Lakein

WHEN YOU DROP MAIL INTO A SLOT outside the post office, nothing happens at first. But soon enough, an employee picks it up and your letter is routed into a vast infrastructure. At incredible speeds, envelopes and packages are scanned, handwriting and printed labels are automatically recognized, and each piece of mail is sorted so it can be passed along to its final destination.

One of the more impressive elements of this system is that it's almost completely invisible. Put a letter in one box, and a few days later it shows up in another box perhaps a thousand miles away.

To regain control of your time, you need the same kind of operation, just on a smaller scale. You need a **task sorting machine.**

And just like the post office, it needs an outside and an inside. Your public entry point—like the mail chute— and the private, internal system where the work is done without most people watching.

And just like the post office, its complexity must be built on rules and policies. Some of these will govern what happens within your system, and others will establish requirements for tasks as they go into the system.

And one great thing about systems is once they work, we don't have to worry as much about the details. [SCT]

You'll have to create your own machine. But you now have the tools to do so. Because you've got the first half of the thesis statement:

> **Predict your emotional energy to optimize your professional experience.**

The last half begins with one word: "optimize." And that's what the post office has done with their system.

It's what you have to do with yours as well.

To understand how to build your own task sorting machine, start with the interior: the deepest, most obscure place in the entire enterprise.

The post office has distribution centers all over the country. Inside one of these massive operations there are areas for letters, for small parcels, and for large packages that have an unusual shape. There's a process for dealing with mail that doesn't have enough postage, or for where the destination address is unclear or incomplete.

You too need distribution points inside your task sorting machine. You need places to keep different kinds of to-process task items. And these places come in three different varieties, which are called **dimensions**.

Physical locations are the most obvious. If you keep paper copies of important files and documents, that's where those tasks are most often accomplished. Examples include your desk at home, the place where you pile incoming mail, your favorite bag for carrying papers and other miscellaneous items, your gym, your favorite coffee shop, and so on.

Virtual locations are what we are all struggling to master in the digital age. This is your email inbox, your text messages, the "desktop" on your computer, a shared drive at work, your digital camera, etc. Many of these are in the so-called "cloud," and accessible from just about anywhere. And others you can only reach with specific passwords or from certain networks.

Temporal locations are spaces in time. That sounds fancier than it is. There are some tasks that are well suited to certain blocks of your day or week. That might be weekday evenings or Sunday afternoons, the first of the month or around the holidays or other specific periods.

It's not easy to make a list of these locations. Our lives are increasingly busy, and we are highly mobile. We have more stuff and more devices. Consider Sara, a professional who shares custody of her three-year-old daughter Myra with Myra's father. Here's a bit of her running internal monologue:

> Get up, it's Tuesday, look for clothes, remember that I picked up my suit from the dry cleaners and it's in the car, go out to the garage in my pjs, get it, bring it back inside. Take shower, brush teeth, get dressed. It's Tuesday, early morning conference call with the overseas office, get number from email on my phone, dial in to listen, put on

makeup while listening. Grab breakfast, we're out of bananas, mental note to add bananas to my shopping list. Conference call over, remember to update report and place on shared drive later today. Go to car, remember that I left my laptop on the dining room table. Go back and get it. Return to garage, start car, but remember it's Tuesday, it's my night with Myra, gotta remember to get Myra's afternoon snack from the fridge. Turn off car, go back inside, get snack, get back in car, go to work. Listen to news, think about the evening, arrive at work, try to remember mental notes, check email, start the day.

There are many locations that Sara uses in this short piece of her day. She has *physical* locations, such as her dining room table (where she worked the night before on her laptop), her car (where she kept her dry cleaning) and her fridge (where she had Myra's snack.)

There are *virtual* locations as well. Sara has to open her email inbox on her phone to get the number for the conference call. She knows she'll need to use the shared drive later in the day. And, Sara makes several "mental notes."

Finally, this whole story takes place on a Tuesday. That is one of Sara's days to be with her daughter Myra. It's also a workday morning, so there are several aspects of her routine impacted by the hustle of getting ready to go to the office. These are all *temporal* locations.

The chaos of Sara's morning is her running from place to place, either in person or in her mind. It's no surprise that she'll have problems later in her day.

Likewise, knowing where you keep the items (and tasks) you need—whether in space, time, or in some kind of information storage—is the first step to building your task sorting machine.

Let's make that list.

Get out three pieces of paper, and label them "physical," "virtual," and "temporal." On each one, start writing down significant places where you keep things and tasks. Here are some examples to consider:

Physical locations:

- The stationery drawer where you keep pens, paper, envelopes and stamps

- Your craft / sewing kit

- The place you file important documents

- The bag you use to transport stuff between locations

- Your car or bus route

- Your mailbox at home or your post office box

- Your favorite coffee shop or bar for working/reading

Virtual locations:

- Desktop computer

- Shared drive at work

- Your online photo storage

- Your email

- Mobile phone

- Your tablet

Temporal locations:

- During business hours (phone calls)

- After business hours

- Weekends only

- Specific days of the week

- Days when your boss is in the office

- Days where the weather outside is nice

Of course you won't include everything. And you will undoubtedly need to come back and add to your lists later. But the point is to begin to define where your work resides so that you can decide how to get it into and out of those systems.

Because what we want is making easy, quick decisions as tasks come to your world, rather than laboring over everything you have to do. *[DPT]*

Once you know your dimensions, it's time to create your systems.

And luckily, it's as easy as 1…2…3.

Suppose your boss comes to your desk. She brings up a small project that she needs completed and asks if you can handle it. You discuss the details and agree to do the work. And then, you figure out when, where, and how you'll complete the task.

This is the **three-stage input system** we should use for any to-do item that comes our way:

1. Receive the information and materials through an incoming stream

2. Acknowledge, decide location, confirm feasibility, and promise an outcome

3. Put the item into the appropriate task queue

To some degree, you already do this whether you realize it or not. *[DPT]* If your spouse asks you to take out the trash, you answer them, decide whether you'll do it then or in a moment or later that day. When it's time you complete the work.

Or do you? It's likely that all kinds of tasks have fallen through the cracks. You may have had good intentions, but distractions, interruptions, or simple forgetfulness may have prevented success.

That's why you need a rigorous three-stage input system for each of the locations within your three dimensions.

It's a lot to build. But like any good operation, each individual piece will become automatic. *[SCT]*

And if you want world-class time management, it has to become as natural as breathing.

To build your three-stage system, start with the inputs for a particular location. What can arrive there? What might you find there if you looked? The input stream is the first step and knowing what to expect sets up the function of this part of your task sorting machine.

For example, if it's a physical location which is a file cabinet in the office, you can probably visualize what is there. You probably know who else (if anyone) puts things into those drawers and takes things out, and the kind of material to expect.

This is true no matter what dimension you consider. If it's the virtual location of the chat program on your work laptop, you know what kind of chatter is typical. If it's the temporal location of your child's weekly soccer practice, you know who you're going to see and how much time you'll have while you wait for practice to be over.

Second, develop an action plan for items in that location, or the best use of the location itself. Acknowledge what is there. Decide what you want to do. Confirm if that action is feasible. And finally, make a promise for a specific outcome.

For example, suppose you're thinking about a physical location: your home mailbox which often gets ignored. **Acknowledge** that it contains junk mail, coupons, bills, and the occasional personal correspondence. **Decide** when you will clear out the box, when you will sort through those categories, what you will keep, and what other physical locations will receive each type of mailing. **Confirm** if you truly have the capacity for that plan—maybe you don't have the resources to look through the advertisements, or you should cancel a few magazine subscriptions. And finally, **promise** yourself that you will stick to this objective.

The same is the case with a virtual location. When an email message arrives, how do you **acknowledge** it? A pop-up or seeing it in your inbox? How do **decide** when and how to process it? How do **confirm** your capacity to respond or to delegate it elsewhere? And what **promise** do you make to others (or yourself) about those messages?

For a temporal location like Saturday mornings or the weekly staff meeting, define a process as well. **Acknowledge** this is a good time to plan out the week or the weekend. Then, **decide** what you're doing with this particular window, and **confirm** if that's feasible given what else you have going on. Make a **promise** to anyone else that might be there about what you're going to do. And move on!

Third, do the work by moving tasks to queues. This could be a pile, a box, or a written list. It could be an electronic folder, or a date on the calendar. This might seem like a waste of time. But a good sorting system doesn't try to do all the work immediately. Instead, each individual item is routed to an area so it can be tackled there—and otherwise forgotten about. *[ZE]*

Think of it this way: if you're cleaning every room in your home, you probably start with picking up loose items, and then perhaps you dust. Finally you sweep or vacuum.

Three stages create a stair-step approach to time management. One staircase for each location: one for the office, one for the laundry room, one for the Sunday you pay bills, and one for the backup drive on the family computer.

When something arrives, you decide which staircase to climb, and never take more than three steps.

Because time management isn't just doing things: it's deciding *when* and *where* to do them.

It's about directing your work through the right three stage task-sorting machine, based on work to be conducted. **Receive** an input. **Plan** what you'll do. **Queue** it to be done. And understand while the machine has three stages, you're doing four micro-tasks to prepare to do the work: **acknowledging** what must be done, **deciding** which physical, virtual, or temporal location is best, checking the **feasibility** of doing this task in your life now, and **promising** when, where, and how it will be done. Or as a visual, imagine each of your machines as looking something like this:

Purpose: *TBD*
Location: *TBD*

1. Acknowledge task
2. Decide location
3. Feasbility check
4. Promise outcome

The insides of these mechanisms are entirely up to you. In our modern lives, that workflow can be highly creative and can be done at anyplace and anytime. But we all know our usual haunts and what time of day we work best. *[CT]* Respect your knowledge of yourself.

Likewise, don't be afraid to create lots of individual machines for each repeatable type of input you have. Consider a pattern for meeting and following up with new contacts, one for reviewing policy documents, one for onboarding new clients, one for processing voicemails, and one for preparing to leave town on business.

Having these handy is like having a chest full of tools. They are innermost gears and levers in the large scale system you're building.

But having the resources is not enough. Just a like a national post office with distribution centers and handling procedures is not enough.

What you need now is the other side: the *outside* of your task sorting machine.

That's the part where everyone else comes into play.

Chapter 7

Outside the Task Sorting Machine

"Someday is not a day of the week."
- Denise Brennan-Nelson

YOU'VE ALREADY GOT THREE-STAGE MACHINES in parts of your life. Without even thinking about it there are places where the process has become so routine it is second nature.

You likely know exactly where to find just about every type of utensil, appliance, plate, saucepan, or gadget in your kitchen. You can walk in the room and see the current state (stage 1), decide if you're going to take action (stage 2), and then get things staged for the next step, such as putting dirty dishes in the sink or groceries in the panty (stage 3).

The act of *entering* the room triggers the decision making progress. *[DWE]* Either you start doing the work, or pile on some mental stress because you're *not* doing it now. *[EGO]*

The challenge in building three-stage systems in the rest our personal and professional lives is that we have even less control and there are even more variables. *[LH]* Plus, we have to do it on purpose. Your pattern for interacting with your kitchen isn't likely something you designed, but rather something that just happened over time.

And in particular, **the problem is other people.** You can't control how people ask you for tasks although you can try. It would be great if everyone in your house at least brought the dishes to the kitchen. It would be helpful if your coworkers could put all direct requests in email instead of shouting them at you as you're heading into the restroom. It would be fantastic if a discussion about rearranging the furniture in the living room could happen while you're at home, instead of hundreds of miles away on vacation.

But people often won't, and so you must adjust.

Just like the post office has to handle people with messy handwriting and incorrect postage, you too must deal with the uncertainty of human beings—regardless of the reason you believe they are this way. *[AT]*

As is the case with many complex systems, the exterior has almost no resemblance to the interior. The post office is willing to accept all kinds of letters, parcels, and packages. You can send things which are tiny and as light as a feather or objects that are too big and too heavy for most people to carry. You can have them deliver money or food or even live animals.

But no matter what you bring in, they will categorize it with only a handful of parameters. Postage is a measure of how much you paid, and how much it will cost them to make the delivery. The type indicates whether this is a letter, a large envelope, or a package. The class specifies how the mail is treated and when it should be expected to arrive. And while there a few more optional components such as tracking and insurance, the post office only needs a few bits of data to characterize the billions of pieces it handles each year.

Your analysis should be the same. Ask yourself: what is the **cost** of this request? What is its **type**? And with what **priority** should I treat it?

These questions allow you to decide which of your three-stage systems to use. Which brings us to the overall picture:

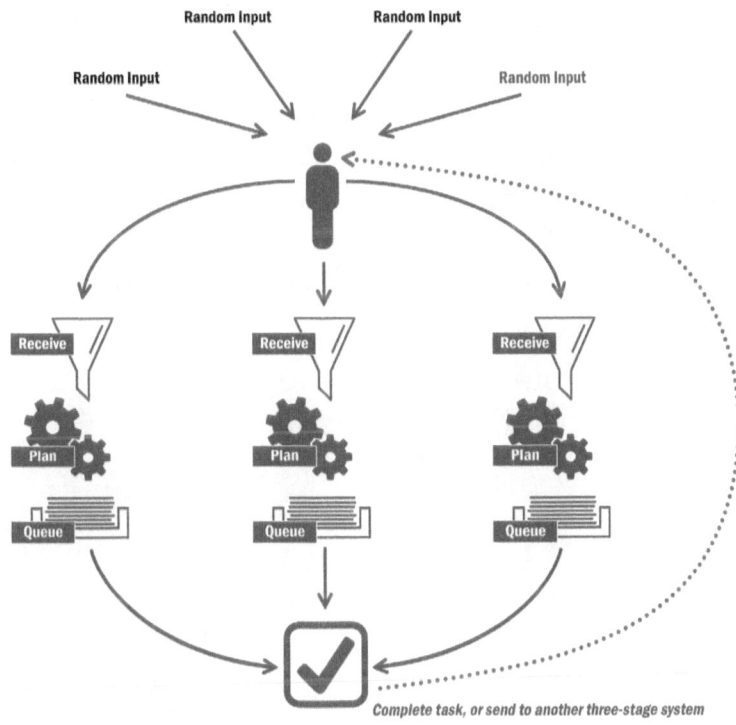

Complete task, or send to another three-stage system

Look through this diagram. You may receive tasks from any number of places: other people telling you what to do, random inspiration striking in the middle of the night, or coming across something that you know you need to tackle.

Like the postal worker behind the desk, you are the first line of defense. You must determine what the **cost** will be to complete this work, the **type** of work it is, and its **priority**. And from there, it can go into one of your many three-stage input systems.

It's worth documenting each three-stage system on a piece of paper. You can draw your own version of the picture, starting with the hopper on the top, the gears in the middle, and the queue at the bottom. Inside the hopper describe the type of work this system is intended to receive. Next to the gears, include the steps in evaluating each item: acknowledging, deciding, determining feasibility, and making a promise. And the set of lines in the queue is a place to write down each of the items that are pending completion.

Purpose: *TBD*
Location: *TBD*

1. **Acknowledge** task
2. **Decide** location
3. **Feasbility** check
4. **Promise** outcome

What happens when something falls out of the queue? You do it. That's the checkbox, the international symbol for "completed." But sometimes the real work is not finishing a task but sending it to a *different* three-stage input system. Being willing to sort and re-sort is what makes your task sorting machine mature and robust.

Visualizing how this might work in your own life isn't easy, because our lives our so complex that a full machine would take an enormous piece of paper to document. But if we just focus on the elements that drive us crazy, the concept becomes manageable and highly useful.

Remember Sara and her daughter, Myra? Imagine an alternate version of her morning:

> Get up, it's Tuesday. On my dresser are my clothes laid out from the night before, including the suit I picked up from the dry cleaners. Take a shower, brush teeth, get dressed.
>
> Go to "home office" on my dining room table where computer is out from the night before. See reminder pop up that today is Tuesday, which means I have Myra tonight and need her afternoon snack, as well as an early morning conference call with the overseas office. Get number from my computer, dial to join call ten minutes early using my headset and leave myself on mute.

Pack up my computer and Myra's snack from the fridge and leave both by the door to the garage. Go to get breakfast. We are out of bananas, write this on the shopping list on the fridge door. I should go shopping tonight; grab shopping list and put with Myra's snack so I remember to go with her.

Conference call starting, put on makeup while listening. Conference call over, need to update report and place on shared drive later today. Use my phone to send myself an email as a reminder. Go to garage and pick up stuff on the way, get in car, listen to news, think about the evening, arrive at work, see my email reminder and update report.

What makes this different? Sara has established multiple three-stage systems for herself. She has one for her work clothes: receive them from the dry cleaner (or her own laundry machine); **acknowledge** what she's going to the office the next day, **decide** what she wants to wear, see if that's **feasible** based on what is clean and what meetings she has for the day, and make **promise** to herself by leaving it on the dresser.

She also has a system for working at her apartment: a "home office" section of her dining room table where she has reminders set up for the next day. She uses the space right by her door to ensure she won't forget anything. She joins the conference early so she doesn't need to keep track of the call-in number and the code. And she even combines her shopping list with her daughter's treat so she will be reminded to go to the store after work.

It's easy to imagine that Sara is calmer, more organized, and more effective as a professional and a mother. She wasted less time and did so by having systems.

Her process included identifying the type of each task as well as the priority. But something Sara didn't tackle was cost.

And in fact, understanding the cost of each task is almost always the hardest part of managing our time. We must address the emotions of the work, estimate the time required, and often, work with others to get things done.

How? It's the next chapter. Onward!

Chapter 8

Operating the Machine

"Destiny is not a matter of chance; it is a matter of choice.
It is not a thing to be waited for, it is a thing to be achieved."
–William Jennings Bryan

MACHINES DO NOT RUN FOREVER. They require maintenance. Moving elements need lubrication. Active components depend upon a source of energy, such as fuel or electricity. Parts will wear out and must be replaced.

And perhaps most profoundly, the **behavior of a machine will vary** based on who is using it. The gentle old lady that only takes her car to church on Sunday will see it last far longer than the frantic sales professional who is logging thousands of miles per week, slamming on the brakes, and pushing past the speed limit.

A task sorting machine, too, operates in accordance with the people who are engaged with it. Furthermore, each person's unique emotional states inform how the invention functions. *[DPT]* We've already discussed multiple affective areas, each of which leads to low or high energy. Here's the chart again:

Low Energy	High Energy
Relief (r)	Regret (R)
Desire (d)	Dislike (D)
Owned (o)	Outsourced (O)
Simple (s)	Skillful (S)
Casual (c)	Challenging (C)

Remember that inventory of all of your current tasks? You ought to be able to look at any one of them and pick answers from the low energy and high energy column. In fact, you can probably do it for all five rows. You'll get something like:

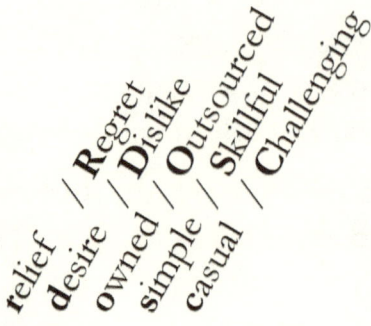

relief / **Regret**
desire / **Dislike**
owned / **Outsourced**
simple / **Skillful**
casual / **Challenging**

- [r D o s c] Go through the junk mail pile

- [R d o s C] Visit a friend in the hospital

- [r D O s c] Fold and put away laundry

- [R D o S C] Study for an upcoming test

- [r d o S c] Write in my journal

- [r d o s c] Send a thank you note

- [r D o s C] Go to gym and exercise

These might not be the choices you would select for these tasks. And you don't even need to pick answers for all five areas. But the exercise demonstrates the emotional impact of the work we *know* we need to do.

And it shows that the task sorting machine isn't as mindless and robotic as one might think. In reality, each time we review a possible task, we face a new mental state as a result. *[DWE]*

To maintain our sanity and maximize our productivity, we should balance low energy tasks with high energy tasks. *[FL]* For every activity that brings us regret, another should be tackled which generates a sensation of relief. Each time we complete a project that we desire we should use that victory to give us the motivation to power through something we dislike.

And when we have the confidence that comes from owning a task and doing it ourselves we can then address the nervousness (and potential time savings) of outsourcing another action to a third party. We can do the same for the quiet joy of a simple task or the energizing focus of one that takes skill, as well as the relaxation that arises from casual work or the excitement of something that challenges us.

The key is balance. High energy and low energy. Calm and chaos. Incidental and intense.

Balance comes from identifying the tasks and placing them into the schedule. Do things not solely in the order of priority, but in a way that gives you both ups and downs.

This is what it means to "Predict your emotional energy to optimize your professional experience."

Start with the tasks you have and determine how each one makes you feel. Then, you can place them on your calendar in the best order possible.

But in order to do that you need to know how much time to allocate to each one.

That's called estimation.

If you want to achieve your goals, you need to break them into tasks. And in order to complete your tasks, you need to schedule them so that you get things done. Otherwise, you'll have an enormous list with no end in sight.

To put a block of work on your calendar, you need to know **when it should be done** and **how long it will take.**

The first question is about emotional impact and priority. Don't schedule a bunch of depressing, challenging, frustrating work for the same day. Don't fill your calendar with easy, fun, engaging work for an entire day either. Mix and match to give yourself momentum, like a roller coaster.

The second issue is about how much time is required. If it's something you've done before, there is little benefit in making an estimate. You can reflect on your memory and block out the period that is needed. You can place it into the hour of the day that best suits your personality, or when you will be in the optimal place and have access to the necessary resources.

But if you've *never* done this task before, it's not a matter of scheduling. Instead, it's about research. You need to think harder about what has to be done and figure out how much time it will take. And that answer might be unknown. *[ICO]*

A good example is troubleshooting a problem. Imagine your car is not working correctly, and you bring it into the mechanic to find the issue. Even the most skilled technician with decades of experience cannot always tell precisely you how long it will take to get you an answer. At best, they can provide a range.

And even if the issue is fixed, the expert may never be able to give you an exact cause. Instead they may be forced to admit they replaced one or more parts that the problem "went away."

Often, the best choice is not to allocate time to complete a task, but to allocate time to study the task to see what it will really take to accomplish.

That means breaking it down into smaller pieces, or perhaps getting help from someone else.

Which may be the most elusive part of time management: **delegating to other people.**

Players may be superstars, but teams win games. Without relying on other people, we cannot accomplish much of anything.

Much of the difficulty in passing work off to others is that we often treat it as a *transaction* rather than an *investment*. If you need someone else to complete a task, you should expect to spend extra time teaching them, coaching them, and correcting early mistakes.

But mostly, it's human psychology working against us. We tend to have a high opinion of our own ability to complete tasks, even if we could hand them off. *[IS]* And when assignments are given to us first it's harder to pass them along. *[EE]*

In order to delegate successfully, it's essential to let go of the experience of the task and embrace the end result. Instead of telling others *how* to do the work, outline *what* it is you want done. That way, they can find their own tools and techniques.

Letting go also means expecting failure to be part of the process. It's not going to go right every time, and that's okay. People need to make mistakes on their own in order to learn. Communicate up front that you understand there will be ups and downs, and if a task is mission-critical, that might not be one you want to delegate.

Lastly, we sometimes try and pass off only things we *don't* want to do. That sounds like a reasonable strategy, until it becomes apparent that someone else is being asked to complete all of the tasks that we find miserable. Even if that's work that doesn't frustrate them, are we really going to respect and value someone who is doing what we farmed out because we disliked it?

Delegate what you enjoy as well as what you detest. Select work that is important, but not crucial. Expect and embrace mistakes. And communicate what you want more than how you want it done.

The results will pleasantly surprise you.

And most importantly, you'll get more done.

Operating a machine often begins with reading the operator's manual. But too often we dive right in, pushing buttons and turning knobs, assuming that it will read our minds and do what we want.

Your own task-sorting machine is unique to you but that doesn't mean you know how to run it. You need an instruction guide. And like most user manuals, at first you'll need to read it in detail. But eventually operating the device will become second-nature.

There are six sections in this imaginary document. Each time you encounter some new input to push through your task sorting machine, you should consider at least one or more the chapters.

Part I is **scope.** A washer is for clothes; a vacuum is for floors. The first step in using your system is to figure out if *you* are the person who is supposed to handle this task. Maybe it should be somebody else, or maybe it can be discarded entirely.

Part II is **impact**. You can grind most anything with an in-sink disposal unit, but some items are better to discard by hand. Likewise, determining the emotional weight of the task is the second step.

Part III is **selection.** There are plenty of ways bring light up a room, but sometimes you want to flip a switch, other times you want to grab a flashlight, and on some occasions use matches and a candle. You too will need to determine which three-stage system will receive the work. And that is dictated by the *cost*, the *type*, and the *priority* of the task at hand—making this the most critical part of the entire process.

Part IV is **estimation**. Everything takes time. If you can specify accurately and precisely how long it will take, you can decide where to put it in your schedule. And if you have no idea, you can use that uncertainty as information as well.

Part V is **capture**. This is your list. It can be a spreadsheet, a sticky note, complex software, or a whiteboard. Whatever you use, save the task, any emotional information you have, the subsystem you'll use, and the time required.

Part VI is **schedule and execute.** This putting it on your calendar and getting it done. Simple.

Remember Sara? Here's how her Tuesday morning at the office might go with these ideas squarely in mind:

> Office cubicle, desk, set down my coffee.
> Coat on the rack, purse in the drawer, phone
> on the charger. There is some mail on my
> chair, but I am not reviewing it that now.

Instead I move it without looking to the bottom of the stack on the inbox bin to the right of my screen.

Turn on the computer and while it starts, take my blank pad and paper. Big items for today: book flight for Vancouver trip. Frank at the front desk can do that. Finish incident report from last week. Ugh, that's going to be painful. It's going to take a lot out of me, and it has to be done today. Work through anonymous employee appreciation submissions for the holiday party. That will be nice, but I could do it later in the week. But I can probably read each one in under 3 minutes and there are 50 to go through.

Okay, computer is on. Looks like there are 72 unread emails since yesterday, and I have a couple of calendar appointments. Do I need to prepare for any of them? The 2pm with Shannon. Better block off time for that now at 1:30pm. I haven't gotten the document to review for the 11am, so I can push David to reschedule.

I'll finish the report first and then read ten evaluations to cheer me up. Then email until lunchtime and then prep for Shannon. And that inbox bin is getting sizable so I'll put aside time this afternoon to tackle that.

I'm ready to face the day.

Sara's experience is about following her own internal instruction manual. For everything that comes her way, she starts with this question:

1. Is this something I **want to do personally,** or just something I want done?
   a. Consider passing that information back to the person who requested the task.
   b. Think: is there is someone better suited to this work?

She has to tackle quite a bit herself. But she pushes making airline reservations over to Frank. And since David hasn't given her the document they are going to discuss, she can have him figure out when to reschedule.

2. Ask **at least one** of the five questions:
   a. Will I feel **relief** of **regret** when I'm done?
   b. Do I **desire** to do this myself or **dislike** the idea of the task?
   c. Is this something I have to **own** or can it be **outsourced?**
   d. Is this task **simple** or does it take some specialized **skills?**
   e. Can I get it done **casually** or will it **challenge** me to use my brain?

Sara is feeling upbeat about reviewing the employee appreciation forms. But the incident report project makes her feel downtrodden. Email is just something to be done. As a result, each item is emotionally classified.

3. Choose the best **three-stage system**.

Here the choices seem almost automatic. Her inbox bin is what receives paper files and mail. Sara's calendar is the best place to reserve time to prep for the afternoon meeting. Most of her routine communication can go into email.

4. Estimate the time it will take from the following list:
    a. Less than two minutes
    b. Less than ten minutes
    c. Less than a half hour
    d. If it's more than that, it's now a ten minute task to break it down into smaller tasks

Because she has many large projects, Sara has to aggressively evaluate how long each one will take. This framework helps her just do what is immediate and schedule out that which takes more time.

5. Write down the task as follows:
    a. A status box
    b. Up to five of the codes (rR/dD/oO/sS/cC)

    c. The time required to do the task (0, 2, 10, 30)

    d. The text of the task as a subject + verb + object

As a fan of written lists, Sara's pad of paper will have checkboxes, a few notes, and some symbols. But of course other people may use a computer-based program as their main system, or visually organize their workspace to remind them of what's next.

In any case, she should repeat the capture process for all of her tasks. And so should you.

6. Schedule significant tasks on your calendar, and then afterwards start knocking things off your list:

    a. Leave as much slack time as you need based on interruptions.

    b. Order the tasks using the codes with an alternation of capital and lowercase letters.

    c. Otherwise use dependency to put them in the proper order.

    d. Otherwise use priority.

Like most professionals, Sara's life is driven by a schedule. She uses her calendar as one of her most important three-stage systems. She knows what she is going to do and when she is going to do it, as far as it is possible to reasonably plan ahead.

If you imagine what's on the page of the user manual for your own task sorting machine, it might look something like this:

I. Scope

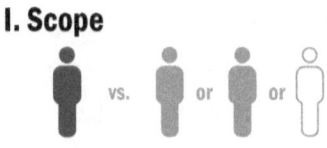

II. Impact

relief vs. Regret
desire vs. Dislike
owned vs. Outsource
simple vs. Skillful
casual vs. Challenging

Appreciated
or
Anxious
or
Angry

III. Selection

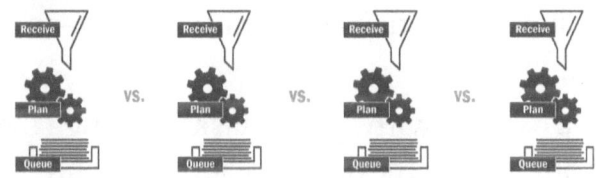

IV. Estimation

V. Capture

☐ Walk the dog at least one mile   rDosc   Home/after work   30m
☐ Request new articles from freelancer rdOSC   Email   20m
☐ Order cake for retirement party   Rdosc   Call/biz hours   2m

VI. Schedule + Execute

A user manual is a well-intentioned document that isn't always reviewed and isn't always useful. All six parts

(scope, impact, selection, estimation, capture, schedule +
execute) may not apply in every situation. But ignore the
instructions at your peril.

You need to develop your own guidelines. Perhaps
you benefit from bullet journaling or legal pads. There
may be software you love for keeping track of your tasks.
Or, you could feel most organized with paper files. Find a
system and a structure that works for you.

If there's an open secret about working complex
machinery, it's that the outcome is often highly dependent
not just on the designer, but the operator. Work with the
tool, keep the parts well-oiled, and use it appropriately—
and it will last a long time. Push it beyond the prescribed
limits, drive it hard, and neglect maintenance—and it will
sputter and die.

It is the same with your task sorting machine.
Understand your own emotional responses and you can
help it purr to life, running flawlessly and efficiently.

Finally, running the machine means doing what
many of us will readily admit we despise: reading the
manual. Yet, the instructions were created precisely for
this purpose.

First, you have to make them.

Then you have to read them. Know them. Live
them.

And adjust them as you learn more and more about the best ways for you to work.

After all, it's your device. It's your time.

And what you do with it is just as important as what you *don't* do.

Build your machine and turn it on.

Chapter 9

Do's and Don'ts of Time Management

"The secret of your future is hidden in your daily routine." –Mike Murdock

THERE'S PLENTY OF ADVICE OUT THERE about how to manage your time. Unfortunately, much of it is contradictory and not well-supported by science or sound thinking. But if you want to create balance and joy in your life, you should predict your emotional energy to optimize your professional experience. This means that understanding the feelings behind each situation will give you more insight than just what to do and not to do.

Category by category, here's what you should pursue and avoid, and why.

Planning

We need to think ahead. One step in winning the game is visualizing the game before you arrive. But there's more to planning than making a promise. There are many areas where you should prepare and others where preparation actually *prevents* success.

DO make a daily list of big items. Start each morning with three to five tasks that you want to accomplish in that day and try and knock them out as quickly as possible. This creates momentum by establishing a sense of accomplishment.

DON'T try and time block every last minute. It is tempting to use your calendar to fill your schedule back-to-back with work. The importance of planning, however, is to create a framework for your objectives, not a rigid set of rules that must be followed. Give yourself space to run over, to daydream, and to respond to urgent, unpredictable requests.

DO divide your time up into smaller chunks rather than larger ones. We tend to be far more precise in predicting shorter periods of time for work. If you have a large task, break it into small pieces. *[GST]*

DON'T estimate time for other people. Instead, let them provide their estimate. Telling someone else how long a job will take removes their agency. Ask them and respect their response.

DO establish daily, weekly, and monthly routines. It's good to brush your teeth daily, to shower on a recurring schedule, and to develop other habits that happen with predictable frequency. Define these and stick to them.

DON'T plan to do something later that you could do right now in under two minutes. If you can fully complete a task the moment it occurs to you, do it immediately. If you can only start the task, save it for later.

DO pay attention to work that is truly urgent. Most everything we need to do can be delayed, but if something must be done as soon as possible, respect that need and make it a priority.

DON'T complete a series of tasks that are easy or fun in a row. Instead, alternate between enjoyable work and necessary but difficult tasks. Establish a pattern of variety in your efforts.

DO batch related tasks together. If you're working alone, it's easier to wash all the dishes, then dry all the dishes, and then put all the dishes away. Structure your own work accordingly.

DON'T keep related items in multiple unrelated places. Establish a single to-do list for yourself. Try to have a single place for incoming items. If you work on multiple computers, get synchronization software that enables you to reach all your data from everywhere.

DO create a backup system for critical data. This should include a process for your digital files and also a secure place for critical paper documents and keepsakes.

DON'T obsess over the tools you use to manage your tasks. The best technology in the world is worthless if you don't use it. A spiral notebook is more than sufficient, as is a spreadsheet. Develop healthy, repeatable patterns first before finding the perfect software application or journal.

Utilization

Merely buying a championship racing bike does not teach you how to ride a bicycle. And even when we know how to use the tools we benefit when we focus on the process. *[OPO]* Pay attention to your utilization of time—not just the fact that you're steadily using it up.

DO shut out distractions. If you need to concentrate, wear headphones, find a conference room, disable the ringer on your phone, or turn down the volume on your computer. Help yourself get things done.

DON'T try and multitask. It is impossible to accomplish more than one significant activity at the same time. The best you can do is rapidly switch between them, which is error prone and inefficient.

DO set up your workspace before you begin. Get everything you need to be productive for a project and lay it out in front of you. That way you don't need to stop to get more materials or resources.

DON'T forget about the tools and experts available to you. As distracting as the Internet can be, it's often the case that someone has done this before and a web search can turn up illuminating and helpful ideas.

DO give yourself frequent breaks—but make them brief. The best way to work is in short bursts followed by short breaks. This is sometimes called the Pomodoro Technique, named after a popular Italian-made kitchen timer shaped like a tomato. Strictly follow the cycle of working and resting to keep yourself moving.

DON'T beat yourself up if you waste time. Instead, forgive yourself and move on. Research led by Dr. Timothy Pychyl indicates that people who practice self-forgiveness after procrastinating tend to reduce the amount of time they goof off the next time around. *[FAE]*

DO vary your body position. Try standing while working, moving to a new chair, or at least taking a break that involves stretching. *[SLA]*

DON'T waste time waiting. Sitting around is part of life, whether you are in line, at the doctor's office, or at an appointment and others have not shown. Always have something to do that is short and productive, such as reading, writing thank you notes, or clearing out old messages.

DO make a list of quick, recurring tasks. These are things you can instead of saying "I don't have time to do anything before this meeting begins", such as clean up your desk, delete old emails, take out the trash, or review your calendar.

DON'T start it without a plan to finish it. That means don't call a customer to chat right before walking out the door! If a task requires more time than you are sure you have right now, put it on your list first and *then* consider if you want to immediately make progress.

Relationships

Managing time requires managing people. But their emotions, needs, and tasks impact what you have to do. Knowing more about them helps you know more about how to manage your own life.

DO take time for people you like. Whether you're introverted or extroverted, we all appreciate good people. Find a way to use their presence to recharge you so you can do more.

DON'T give your time to people you don't like. The best way to complete a request from someone you can't stand is to do it anywhere except near them. Create distance so you don't get drained by energy vampires.

DO have something to do when people are late. When someone's running behind, you're either going to be annoyed, indifferent, or relieved. But in any case, always have simple tasks to complete, such as reading a book, writing thank you cards, clearing out voicemails, or reviewing your calendar. This helps reduce the chance that their lateness will become your resentment. *[FR]*

DON'T run over your appointment times. Unless you've successfully communicated to everyone in your life that start and end times are fluid, staying too long in an appointment will only create a chain reaction in the lives of people around you. Be firm and wrap things up!

DO tell people when the task is trivial for you. As an expert in your field, there are some tasks that will take longer for another person to describe out loud than for you to complete! Help establish their understanding for how much time work requires.

DON'T rush the deadline or pad the schedule. We sometimes overpromise to try and curry favor or give ourselves extra time "just in case." This is dishonest, and when you get caught, you get burned. Instead, explain the timeframe and include the contingencies.

DO pay careful attention to how others waste your time. It's much easier to notice your time being wasted than to realize you're chewing up someone else's day. Learn from the mistakes of others. *[AT]*

DON'T say "yes" to everything. Responding with "no" is empowering as it shows a loyalty to your profession rather than your boss and it helps you to have balance in your life. If you have trouble declining work then try trading it for something that would be easier to complete. *[SDB]*

DO communicate what was required. Or in other words, don't labor in secret. The more you complete behind the scenes, the less others know to value your time. And worse, they may wonder if you padded the schedule because they didn't see you working.

DON'T use a relationship to get an answer you can get yourself. Have a question? It's often easy to pop your head over a cubicle wall, send a text, email, or instant message. But if you can find out yourself by doing a little research, asking another person might negatively impact the relationship.

DO let people know what you found. Discover a clever trick or workaround? Get an answer that might help others in the future? Share it with others to build your relationships.

DON'T use assumptions to make excuses. If you think someone else doesn't know how, is too busy, or wouldn't want to do it *[AT]*, you might decide to tackle the job yourself. But if you find out first, you may be able to collaborate or delegate the task instead.

DO pay attention to people's lives. Don't be a gossip, but be aware of what's going on with your colleagues, friends, and fellow volunteers. If they are preparing for their daughter's wedding or spending the evenings with their best friend in the hospital, they might be a little distracted. Adjust accordingly.

DON'T be afraid to let others fail. People need to make mistakes in order to learn. *[SCT]* Tell this to others before passing off work, and be understanding when things go wrong. And most importantly: resist the urge to rescue people who are struggling. Vanquishing a tiny bit of fear on their own will build their confidence.

Motivation

Getting things done requires that you, personally, find the drive to keep moving forward. That's motivation. To paraphrase Zig Ziglar, motivation is like bathing: it must be employed regularly to be effective.

DO give yourself small treats. There is broad scientific consensus on three aspects of self-motivation: it works well if 1) you set up your own reward system, 2) if the positive bumps occur with considerable frequency, and 3) the benefits are modest but meaningful. Try candies or nuts, one for each small task completed. Or, reward yourself by starting the next song on your playlist. *[CC]* *[DG]*

DON'T punish yourself or engage in negative-self talk. Self-forgiveness is far more effective than self-shaming. If you don't meet your goals, acknowledge that you are not perfect, that you do try hard, and that you'll renew your efforts in the future. *[LH]*

DO celebrate big wins. Small victories might deserve a tiny piece of chocolate or a quick text message to a friend. Major achievements should be followed by celebrations. Take yourself out to see a show, get a great meal, or buy yourself that gift you've been thinking about. You did it; you deserve it! *[GE]*

DON'T get hung up on small details. A motivation killer is when one particular detail isn't quite right. Even if you're not someone who usually needs everything to be perfect, we can all become obsessive-compulsive for a moment and lose our drive. Let that detail go and move on to something else! *[DPT]*

DO meditate and center yourself. Plenty of research shows that mindfulness practices such as yoga, silent reflection, prayer, and meditation help to reduce stress and increase concentration. *[MFL]* For a quick mini-boost, set a timer for 60 seconds, close your eyes, focus on your breathing, and clear your mind.

DON'T deprive yourself of sleep. Think of rest as an investment in yourself that must be paid on a daily basis. Need a few more hours in a day? You can skimp on that transaction by going into sleep debt, but the interest is absolutely brutal. Rest when you're supposed to, and especially when you're tired. Take naps when you need extra focus. *[SEL]*

DO exercise and eat well. Alternate between sitting and standing. Be physically active and consume a balanced diet. Your ability to manage your time requires your brain to be well-fed and supported, which starts with your body. You know what to do!

DON'T work in only one environment. Motivation requires stimulation and changing what you see around you helps keep those synapses firing. Relocate to a conference room, a picnic table, or a coffee shop. Recommend an off-site retreat. And if you work from home, try moving to a different room. Variety motivates. *[CF]*

DO be humble. Studies show that if you think that you're more productive than people around you that can lead to justifying goofing off and less productivity! *[ML]* Instead, acknowledge that while you are getting things done you can always improve.

DON'T ignore your own natural cycles. Science has known for decades that people have circadian rhythms that predict when they do their best work. *[CT]* These change with age and to a degree are unique to individuals.

Don't feel like you have to get up early if that doesn't work for you.

You know what to do. You know what *not* to do.

But not everyone does. And even if they did, knowing something and putting it into action are two entirely different things.

To see the new science of time management in the real world, find the story that works for you.

That's what's next.

Chapter 10

The Administrative Assistant

"Those who are happiest are those who
do the most for others." –Booker T. Washington

FOR OVER FIVE YEARS, Nathan had worked in that law office, supporting seventeen different attorneys. He handled their schedules. He reviewed their correspondence. He fielded phone calls from clients in all kinds of emotional states. And even though his title said "Administrative Assistant" he sat in the front of the building, working as a receptionist, mail carrier, and office manager.

"You might think the partners are the worst," Nathan would explain to friends outside the office. "By all rights, they should be. They have the most high-profile cases, they are bringing in the most money, and they are working the craziest hours."

"But it's the associates. And the paralegals. They are constantly asking me to do things, and it seems like *everything* is due yesterday. Get this couriered over to the courthouse. Put together this mailing. Set an appointment with this client. Order me this for my office. It's a lot of *this this this.*"

Nathan could find plenty of things to complain about. There wasn't much room for advancement, for example. He barely had the authority needed to do much of his job. And while he had a few people he got along with, most of his coworkers were curt and dismissive.

If there was one thing he could control, however, it was how he managed his own time. Nathan resolved to make changes, one by one, to see if it made a difference. He started with how he answered the telephone.

❖ ❖ ❖ ❖ ❖

Nathan didn't have any trouble remembering his first week on the job. [AE] He overlapped with Janine, the woman who was retiring after nearly three decades in the seat he now held. She eagerly explained how their system worked. "I always just answer the phone when it rings, and I say the same thing. 'Stratton and Simon, how may I help you?'"

She showed him how to transfer to other extensions. She mentioned which staff members like to screen calls, and which ones didn't. She taught him how the hold feature worked for when more than one person was calling at the same time.

It wasn't hard, and Nathan mastered the system in a few days. Within the first couple of weeks, he knew enough about all the employees to know how to handle incoming calls. But all of that knowledge didn't solve the fact that the phone seemed to buzz endlessly.

And for Nathan, the phone was a constant annoyance. It seemed to have an almost magical power to ring when he was trying to get something done.

A sizable percentage of those phone calls involved case files, which had 11-digit number that he could *almost* remember long enough to pull from the archives without writing them on a post-it note. [ML]

So one Monday, he counted. Nathan took out a sticky note and made a tick mark for each inbound call. By the closing time the phone had rung 67 times.

On Tuesday, he made some changes. There was no need to answer on the first ring, he figured, and so if he was working on something else, he resolved to keep going until the third ring to pick up the extension.

This small change had a huge impact on Nathan's attitude. It was as if he was saying to that noisy box: "I will help you, but I will finish helping *me* first." It was only an extra ten seconds, but those seconds belonged to him. He found that short moment of control gave him motivation and a sense of calm.

Nathan found an index card to use for case files numbers. He hand-printed the ten most common two-digit prefixes on the card, and then laminated it. That gave him enough time to grab a dry erase marker and finish the remaining nine digits when somebody started firing off one of these codes.

Something else occurred to Nathan as well: anyone calling the office didn't know if there were other people on the line. He added a new script to his repertoire. "Stratton and Simon, this is Nathan. Would you mind holding for just one moment?"

It wasn't necessary for every inbound call. In fact, he tended to reserve it for when the display implied it was a telemarketing company. Or sometimes, when he needed just another 30 seconds to finish an email or wrap up some other project. But those completions added up. In fact, Nathan felt less interrupted than ever before. And by the end of the week, he felt far more productive.

"It's not just that I am getting more done," Nathan would explain to anyone outside the office that would listen. "It's that I *know* I'm going to get more done. I'm that much more in control and that much more confident."

There were more time management ideas he put into use with the telephone. After some variation, his opening script became "Stratton and Simon, this is Nathan speaking. Can I be of service, or may I direct your call?"

Nathan's choice felt empowering. And it also shortened the response time, since half of the people calling only did so because they did not have their contact's direct number. That made Nathan realize that with permission from individual staff members, he could give out those numbers. And that led to a precipitous drop in the overall front desk call volume.

With the phone under control, Nathan turned his attention to other areas. Although the office had modern computer systems, the practice of law was still heavily dependent on paper. Attorneys and paralegals were constantly sending and receiving written correspondence. Since Nathan had the stamps in his drawer and because he worked by the entrance, he managed postal mail for the firm.

Mail came in two varieties, Nathan reasoned: incoming and outgoing. For mail that arrived each afternoon, he would take the bundles and walk around the office, dropping it on people's desks. This didn't take long unless the recipient had their door closed. In that case, he'd make a second run later in the day.

For outbound mail, Nathan received it in all varieties. Sometimes people would bring it by his desk, ready to go except for a stamp. In other cases, he would receive a letter by email, be told to print it, and then send it out. And for some projects he would be given a group of addresses to receive a form letter. Depending on the person asking and how disorganized they were in their request, this might become an all-day project.

Just *thinking* about mail created some anxiety in his mind. When it was urgent, the mail couldn't get to the recipient fast enough. Some of the employees of the firm would bark at him if he didn't deliver incoming letters and packages immediately or didn't prioritize their outgoing projects. But later, the very same people would ignore mail on their desk for weeks or not bother to get Nathan the information he needed to send out a few letters. It was infuriating.

Nathan decided that outgoing mail was more complex and he would tackle it first. Because someone came to him several times a week with a letter in want of stamp, he moved them from his desk drawer to a visible location. Each time someone dropped by in need of postage he politely showed them the new storage spot and encouraged them to apply it themselves. Within a month, practically everyone was peeling-and-sticking without his assistance, and most didn't even interrupt his workflow—and if Nathan was away from his desk they handled it themselves!

There was something freeing about having people come by your desk, quietly take a stamp from the small box at the corner and drop their own letter in the outgoing mail bin. Nathan felt like he had *made* something. In this one small way people were working for *him*.

Having that sense of authority gave him enough pride to try something else that was a bit more sensitive. Outgoing mail also included people who sent him an email with an attachment and the instructions "please print and mail." Admittedly, this didn't take long to complete. Nathan had a printer on a file cabinet by his desk and when he caught the email, he'd use that machine to produce a hardcopy of the letter. He even had a small label printer for the address, so a quick copy/paste saved him the trouble of lettering it by hand.

Both of these devices were on the office network. Nathan asked the IT provider for Stratton and Simon if the printers could be made available to other users. He also asked to have their names changed from the generic make and model number provided by the manufacturer to "Printer for outgoing postal letters (front desk)" and "Printer for mailing labels (front desk)."

It took time and patience, but Nathan steadily trained everyone in the office to use the printer when they wanted to send a letter. He convinced them it would be faster, since it didn't require him to check his email, and also more precise. For Nathan it was easy: whenever he heard the printer start, he would stuff the letter in an envelope. And if he left his desk for a moment, he would check the tray whenever he returned.

The label printer was much more difficult. Special software was needed, and most people didn't want to use it. But a few of the more tech-savvy employees liked it, and Nathan's efficiency improved. It kept his email focused, and the added time of writing a few addresses by hand was far outweighed by the time saved.

There was one last outgoing mail problem, and it was a doozy: mail merge projects. For these Nathan would get an email or a visit from someone describing a group of recipients who should all be sent the same letter, except with different names and address blocks. In the best case scenario, these would come as spreadsheets with all of the details included. But often it would be an email with a list of names. Nathan would have to look each one up in their client database to find the address. And sometimes it was worse; a partner would give him a stack of handwritten notes and he'd have to figure it out. Sometimes it took the better part of a week to get one completed.

It wouldn't be possible to manage all of these situations with one unified system. But Nathan started by creating a form that he distributed to the staff. Because he wanted to make it clear that this tool was optional but advantageous, he explained that any requests for mail merge would be completed within one business day—but only if they used the form. It included a link to a spreadsheet template on the office's shared drive.

It worked. People started using the document and Nathan found himself with more time. This allowed him to tackle incoming mail. For years he had thought about researching possible options for mailboxes. He wanted to go through office supply catalogs and scour the Internet. But this had always seemed like something he could never justify—until now.

Nathan's solution was an elegant, attractive set of vertical metal folders that hung in the breakroom. He marked each one with the name of one person in alphabetical order and was particularly pleased with himself that he chose a unit whose labels could be moved. That way if a person joined or left the office, he could maintain alphabetical order without much trouble.

The mail station went up without incident and many people started using it right away. Nathan would make a second pass near the end of the day to personally deliver items, but this soon became unnecessary. After all, everyone wanted their mail, and they knew where it was.

And since there was more time, there was more opportunity for Nathan. Before, his week was a constant scramble. Now, he had freed up hours ad hours for bigger projects and contributions.

People began to notice. And a few months later, Nathan was in a meeting with the partners at Stratton and Simon, who wanted to offer him a raise.

It should be no surprise that Nathan's story is about time management. But it's also about emotional energy. He knew how people around him made him *feel*. Whether it was the same person calling for the third time in one day, or a paralegal that needed to send out twenty letters on a moment's notice, his relationships dominated his ability to manage his time.

Nathan's change is the mantra:

Predict your emotional energy to optimize your professional experience.

No matter what your position in the organization, you have the ability to contemplate how events and people will impact you.

No matter how many times you must give up your concentration because the phone rings or someone visits your desk, you have the power to choose a plan for your reaction.

We cannot predict the future. But if we've seen the pattern enough times we can prepare.

If you're like Nathan and are being pulled in a million directions, let the rhythm be your guide.

Be ready, and forge ahead.

Chapter 11

The Overbearing Boss

"A bad system will beat a good person every time."
–W. Edwards Deming

ELSIE'S TITLE WAS "PROJECT MANAGER" but in private she would describe her job as "cat herder." In truth, there was only one individual she had to wrangle on a daily basis: her supervisor, Ralph. The way he ran the department drove Elsie crazy more days than not, and it was starting to impact her sanity.

Ralph wasn't a mean person. In fact, he could be spontaneously kind. When they wrapped a big project the year before, Ralph gave Elsie and her husband a gift certificate to a fancy downtown restaurant. And it wasn't just once in a while. He'd sometimes wander into her cubicle at four o'clock on a Friday afternoon, note that it was a beautiful day outside and insist she should go home early.

But Ralph's moods were inconsistent. Although he was generally effective, his emotional variability made for a difficult working environment. At times Ralph would become obsessed with details, micromanaging every aspect of Elsie's work. At other times he would be so distant that he wouldn't respond to emails for weeks, and Elsie would have to run the risk of making decisions on her own.

Not that Elise minded making decisions, of course. It was the repercussions if that choice happened to be one that Ralph wanted to control.

Many of Ralph's problems came down to disorganization and lack of focus. He would give Elsie tasks to do with nearly impossible deadlines, despite the fact that the work had been sitting on his own desk for months before he ever mentioned it. And if he was working late because he was behind on a project, he expected that she should be working late too—along with everyone else on the team.

Ralph's office doubled as the company conference room. But the large table was always covered with papers (and Ralph was always interrupting meetings.) Nobody wanted to say anything *[BYE]* which meant that topics that could have been resolved through group discussion ended up in long email chains.

But many of the issues were about Ralph's ego and his desire to be in control. Although Elsie was the expert on the company's project management software systems, Ralph would get frustrated when things "took too long" to do. That, in turn, hurt Elsie's feelings, because she knew he didn't understand the complexity involved in some of his requests.

Work productivity improved significantly when Ralph was on vacation, but not when he was out of the office to see clients. He would call the office to "check in" and interrupt Elsie and others, and even ask questions about his own travel schedule! Worst of all, Ralph would get angry if people didn't answer, despite his own use of caller ID as screening tool. *[CD]*

With all of these challenges, Elsie was on the verge of trying to find another job. But she decided to give it one last shot. Here's what she did.

During a heartwarming conversation with a dear friend at lunch, Elsie realized that her calendar was the first line of defense against Ralph's moodiness.

"This has been great," she asked at the end of the meal. "Can we make this a standing date? Every Tuesday, here at this restaurant, at noon?"

The idea was met with a smile. "Sounds perfect!"

The weekly lunch became a focal point around which Elise scheduled the rest of her work. She adjusted her most contentious meetings with Ralph to be immediately before, so she had a reason to leave them on time. Elsie put time-consuming, almost mindless projects immediately after, because the pleasant lunchtime conversation gave her the momentum to push through.

Tuesdays from noon to one became a pivot point for her. As a bright spot in her week, it meant that she always knew she'd be in a good mood. And with her improved attitude, she realized she could put positive feelings to good use.

One Friday, Ralph came into her cubicle. "I just got back from an offsite meeting," he told her. This wasn't news to Elsie, because Ralph had told her he was leaving in the first place, and had her prepare some materials just in time for him to depart. But she smiled anyway.

"And it's just beautiful outside, Elsie. You should take off early."

This time, Elsie was ready. "You know what, Ralph, I could use some fresh air. I think I'm going to take a walk outside. Thank you for the suggestion."

This wasn't directly acquiescing to his request. She wasn't leaving for the day. But Ralph still felt like he was heard, and he watched Elsie grab her purse and notepad and head for the door.

A block from the office, Elsie took a seat on a park bench. She pulled out her notepad and allowed her mind to wander. Away from the bustle of the office—and with Ralph's encouragement to go outside—it was easy for her to dedicate time to thinking broadly.

Basking in the sunshine, she made lists. Pros and cons of recent events, regular tasks on her plate, and notes about her own strengths and weaknesses. As a result, several ideas came to mind that made sense for working with Ralph and to become a better project manager in general.

First, Elsie had already seen the success of the weekly lunch date with her best friend. She identified other tasks that brought her joy. Updating the Gantt charts that showed the visual representation of each project was something that she liked doing. She also appreciated her weekly status calls with three of their clients, mainly because those projects were going well.

What she didn't enjoy was also easy to list: processing expense reports for the off-site consultants, dealing with a client where the project wasn't going well, and a bunch of crazy, last-minute things that Ralph dumped on her desk.

With a little further reflection, Elsie realized that there was more to her work than just what she enjoyed and did not enjoy. Updating the team documentation brought her momentary happiness but didn't help spike her energy for the rest of the day like talking to happy clients. And processing expense reports was annoying, but not really something she dreaded.

Elise committed to stacking her calendar accordingly. She even made a plan to reach out to her clients in the next week to see if she could move the standing phone calls to times that would be better for the emotional ups and downs of her schedule.

And she came up with another idea that made her smile. Elsie resolved to put in place immediately.

It was Monday morning, and Elise was getting a jump on the week.

"Hi Ralph," she typed, opening an email message. "I know you're extremely busy right now, so I'd want to suggest we have Bill to take the sales call for Burgess & Graydon on Friday. If I don't hear from you by Wednesday at noon, I'll assume this is fine. Thanks!" *[DCE]*

Then she added a calendar appointment for Wednesday at noon to remind herself and moved on. If she had asked Ralph his opinion, he might have gotten into a discussion with her about the best person to send. But by being proactive, all Ralph had to do is *not* respond. And with his general behavior, him *not responding* wouldn't be all that surprising!

Email was Elsie's new toolbox for engaging with her boss. When he called in that Wednesday from the airport, she answered the phone differently than usual.

"Hey Ralph, I'm glad you called, I was just sending you an email right now with a status update. If you want to give me a minute to finish it then you can read it on the plane."

"Thanks, Elise!" was his response. "I appreciate you being proactive."

"My pleasure. You know I was thinking, if this is helpful to you perhaps we could create a process to send out a quick daily update by email for all of our projects. You can pass them along to the executive team as needed, and you'll have a written record handy."

"That sounds like a good idea!"

And with that, Elsie had a new system in place for reducing Ralph's interruptions. By playing preemptive defense, she could be ready to dodge the unexpected variability that would so often derail her day.

Within a few months, the patterns in the office started to change. At first Ralph continued to pop in with questions, but once he realized they were being handled through existing systems it was harder for him to justify the visits.

And that meant all that was left were his misconceptions about schedules and deadlines. The eternal optimist, he wanted everything done faster than was possible. Ralph wanted to wow customers and impress the company owners.

But as the old saying goes, you can't cook ten-minute rice in one minute—even if you have ten stoves and ten cooks working on the project. With more time to discuss these items with him, Elsie found ways to get him engaged in setting reasonable schedules and deadlines.

Part of this was engaging him more in the process, showing him her charts and documentation. This helped Ralph to have a greater sense of trust that she knew what she was doing.

But even more important were the regular progress updates. Because Ralph got them from Elsie before he could ask, he always felt like he was the one learning and that the team didn't need encouragement or someone checking on them.

Ralph could do what he did best: build new client relationships, rather than trying to manage projects. And in turn, Elsie got to do more of what she enjoyed.

Her plan to look for a new job turned into something better: expanded responsibilities and a raise to match. And even though she didn't need them as much anymore, she kept her Tuesday lunches.

Because the routine made the difference.

Elsie went from wanting to quit her job to being better at it than ever. She found a way to manage her boss by understanding how his actions made her feel.

She internalized this idea, and made changes accordingly:

> **Predict your emotional energy to optimize your professional experience.**

Elsie realized that there were many routine tasks that she could schedule more effectively to help her feel better about work. But the main emotional driver was her boss, Ralph. By modifying *her* patterns, she modified *his* behavior.

By her being proactive, it was harder for him to inadvertently ruin her day.

That's why it's essential to think about how people make you feel and figure out what you can do to influence their behavior.

Because Ralph is a good person, even if he's not a naturally a good boss.

And knowing how to manage the people around you is essential to learning how to manage your own time—and manage yourself.

Even if you feel like you have no time left at all.

Chapter 12

The Exhausted
Account Manager

"Nothing can change until we do."
–Earl Nightingale

AMIT DIDN'T START OUT TO BE A SALESMAN. That's not even what his business card says. He's an "account manager," and often Amit thinks of himself as someone who does nothing but try to juggle those accounts.

With 53 different clients on his list, there's always something. And with his company's product—an online portal for warehouse inventory management—it feels like there's never enough time in the day.

"You're the first line of defense," Amit's future supervisor told him in the job interview. "Account managers are sales guys, but they are also customer support representatives."

"And therapists," he laughed. "And friends. But parents too, because you have to draw the line sometimes."

Amit would readily admit that he had to play all those roles, often in the same day. He was pulling fifty and sixty hour weeks. He knew something had to change. But what?

The total number of accounts was not something that Amit had at the top of his mind until he took the trouble to count. His employer did have software that helped him keep track of open support requests and an accounting department kept him up-to-date on billing, but it wasn't until he sat down to create a spreadsheet that he realized the scope of his responsibility.

The document grew from just customer names to include key contacts and the features they were using. Amit wondered what else could he add? On a quiet Friday afternoon, Amit made a list of additional columns to place on his master spreadsheet:

- Last time he talked to this client

- If he thinks they are happy with the product

- Easy or difficult work with

- How they prefer to be contacted

- Types of issues they typically have

It didn't take long for Amit to fill out the spreadsheet with these columns for the data he had. He was consistent with his data so it was easy to sort and filter.

That gave Amit totally new ways to look at all of the accounts he managed. He was able to focus in on specific subsets, like the clients who he had not talked to in over a month. If he was working late, he could filter clients by those who preferred email, so he could respond then.

And more importantly were the blanks in the document. There were some clients that Amit didn't know how they felt about the company's product or his service. For those, he could send a survey or ask them on the next call.

Getting this document up-to-date gave Amit a sense of accomplishment. For the first time in months, he felt like he had a handle on things—even if he still had a ton of work ahead of him.

And that's when he began to change his patterns.

The first thing he did was acknowledge the clients he enjoyed talking to. There were 14 of them, 12 of which were happy to chat on the phone. Having that list at the ready meant that Amit always knew what to do when he was having a rough time.

When another one of his accounts sent an angry email or called to complain, Amit used to get frustrated or feel like quitting his job.

But now, he'd check his list of the top customers and see which one he had not spoken to in the longest time. Amit would give them a ring to check in, and they'd be happy to hear from him. The positive vibes outweighed the negative energy from the previous customer and gave Amit the ability to focus and resolve their problem.

At first, this was an effective way for Amit to balance out his day. But after a while, he realized that just looking at his list of satisfied customers made him feel better. He didn't need to make a call on every occasion.

In fact, his new goal became the plan to expand the list of happy customers. How could he solve problems, correct past issues, and help things improve?

Each Monday, Amit would pick a client where he wanted to improve the relationship. He might send them a small gift or give them a special offer. Most of the customer service requests didn't come in until the afternoon anyway, so this was a good way to start the week.

That Monday pattern inspired more structured events in the week. On Wednesday afternoons, Amit would pick a client at random and send them a handwritten card in the mail. He marked the spreadsheet so that he didn't repeat anyone. It would take a year to get through the full client list, but how often do you get something in the mail from your account rep?

And then Amit came up with a new plan. It would be a Friday morning task, and it would be a review of the week. How much time was he spending on each client? How much frustration were they generating?

The spreadsheet became richer. It started to track history as well as status. And then, Amit came up with his boldest idea yet. He presented it to his boss in their annual review.

"I've got the data, and these three clients are costing us the most money for the least return." He explained. "If you consider what they are paying and how much time we're spending on them, we actually are *losing* money."

"Really?" his boss replied.

"Yeah, check out the spreadsheet." Amit showed how if you added up his time as well as the engineering team's support work, all three of these clients were quite expensive.

"What do you want to do?"

"I'd like to reassign two of them to other reps, to see if they can get a better response. But for the last one, I think we should fire them. They really aren't a good fit for what we offer."

This wasn't the kind of thing Amit would have felt comfortable saying without the data. It wouldn't even be something he could have said without the renewed confidence of the past six months. But most importantly, Amit was ready to suggest the change based on some other data he'd collected.

"You'll see that I've added 11 new clients since our last review. And based on the data, all of them are happy and highly profitable."

Because, Amit explained, the systems in his spreadsheet allowed him to better understand prospects. He knew what questions to ask based on what kind of customers he's already seen. He knew to find out how they prefer to be contacted, what types of issues they would face, and what would keep them satisfied.

His data made the difference.

Most professionals understand the basics of spreadsheets. Putting data into rows and columns helps us keep organized. But Amit fully committed to the idea when his work life was getting out of control.

It was acknowledging how the angry clients made him feel that inspired him to call the ones who he liked.

It was categorizing client preferences and experiences that made him realize what he could do to improve his relationships.

It was seeing the data clearly for the first time that let him plan ahead.

Amit embraced the idea:

> **Predict your emotional energy to optimize your professional experience.**

If you're overwhelmed, you can do the same.

And there may be no one who has more going on than someone trying to create a new business from the ground up.

Chapter 13

The Distracted Entrepreneur

"You can always find a distraction
if you're looking for one." –Tom Kite

THE DREAM HAD BEEN WITH JACKSON for as long as he could remember. But taking the plunge to start his own business as a nutrition coach was almost nothing like he anticipated.

Back when he was still at the hospital in his job as a charge nurse, he'd catch himself daydreaming. *[MC]* He'd have a little case of his favorite supplements that he took to appointments. He visualized himself at the grocery store with clients, helping them pick out meals. He'd imagine his monthly cooking class or talking with people who had special dietary needs.

But when he approached his boss and went to part-time at the hospital, most of "Life System Nutrition Services, Inc." was anything but what he had predicted. In fact, much of it was stuff he had no idea how to do.

Between issues with incorporation, figuring out insurance, and dealing with vendors, Jackson quickly found himself mired in paperwork and phone calls. And he knew he needed business cards, a website, and probably other marketing materials.

Getting organized meant knowing what he had to do. And all the while, his savings were disappearing fast.

While he had no basis for comparison, Jackson was under the impression that it would be easier to buy a franchise rather than start from scratch. But that meant going to training in another state. It required a small business loan, which was anything but simple. And much to his surprise, it involved a bunch of decisions he never expected to make.

One of the most impactful choices was the decision not to get a dedicated phone line for his business. *My cellphone will be fine*, he reasoned. Why incur the extra expense when he didn't realistically expect to be able to have enough revenue to cover his costs for six months?

But then, the calls started coming in. Every time it rang, Jackson went into a panic. Would this be a new customer wanting to book a consultation? Would it be the franchise office asking for more information? Maybe it was his bank, or his accountant, or one of three different insurance companies. And sometimes, it might even be a friend or family member calling to say hello.

The phone wasn't Jackson's only problem. He quickly came to the realization that his biggest distraction was his own brain.

He'd catch himself fantasizing about some aspect of the business while in the car and miss an exit.

He'd be running through a mental list of what someone had said at the training and start to second-guess what he still had to do.

And sometimes he'd be walking down the hallway at the hospital in the middle of his part-time job, and some critical piece of information would strike him like lightning. And then, perhaps later that day or even a day or two later, he'd struggle to remember that thought.

In short, Jackson was stressed.

So, he decided to get organized. He went to the mall and headed into a stationery store. He took his time, finding a notebook that was the right size and shape. He ran his fingers across the material and the binding, trying to sense if he really would carry it everywhere. He selected one with an attached loop for a pen and picked out a quality writing instrument to match.

And then he went to the register with his choice. "I only found the one. Do you have any more in stock like this?"

Jackson had selected a pad that was exactly the right size to fit in the pocket on his nursing scrubs. He carried it everywhere. To the kitchen, to his bedside table, in his car, and during work.

That pad became the place to save any information that came to him. He'd stop in his tracks and jot something down. He'd pull off the road into a parking lot to make a note. Getting the data out of his head was crucial .*[ZE]*

The second habit he developed was getting the notes from his pad into something else. It took a while, but eventually Jackson made a spreadsheet on his computer. It wasn't pretty, but it did become more and more organized over time.

Developing this system for himself had a tremendous impact on his stress level. Instead of feeling constantly overwhelmed, Jackson felt he had a handle on most of his business life. Instead of panicking, he could work.

And then, he turned his attention to the phone.

At first, Jackson wanted to buy a second cellphone. He'd seen this done by other professionals, and it felt like an easy solution.

Every call on the second phone would be for his business. The voicemails would be separate, but he could return them on an as-needed basis.

But a conversation with a friend turned him around.

"Jackson, you could do that anyway. You can always return messages. That's not the problem; it's that you aren't getting to stuff that matters fast enough."

The discussion led to a new idea. Instead of changing his own behavior, Jackson wondered if he could modify the behavior of other people. He recorded a new message on his cellphone.

"Hello, you've reached Jackson at Life System Nutrition Services. Due to the nature of my work providing individualized, one-on-one nutrition coaching to clients, I am often not able to return phone calls until the following business day. If you need me urgently, you can text this number, or you can email me at jackson at life systems dot com."

It didn't work on everyone. But it started having an impact pretty quickly. Jackson could answer emails early in the morning, and he was even able to respond to voice messages often by switching them to emails.

And that's when Jackson took his systems to the next level.

With the phone calls reduced and his ideas more effectively managed using his notepad, Jackson slowly began picking up a few clients. Most of them were friends and family, but a few were calling his cellphone thanks to the online marketing efforts provided by his franchise.

Unfortunately, his callbacks weren't always resulting in an appointment. Jackson reached out to another franchise owner who had been assigned as a mentor to ask for advice.

"When people call for nutrition help", he explained, "they are usually feeling their need right at that moment.

If you call them back the next day, they may not even recognize your number! Or, they may have found help elsewhere."

The feedback made sense. Jackson didn't need a whole other phone to carry with him. He needed another number—one just for business—that would always be answered.

And while he didn't like the idea at first, he realized that this was something he could outsource. After a bit of research, he found an answering service that would take calls, set appointments, and send him an email with any other details.

And steadily, his business grew. In a few months, Jackson went to his boss at the hospital to tell him what he'd been looking forward to for years.

"It's time for me to resign so I can focus on my business full-time."

Jackson had a problem that many of us have experienced. His life was stressing him out.

But he was willing to stop and analyze why that was happening. What was upsetting him? What was exciting him?

For Jackson, those feelings made it hard to see his dream come true. But again, here it is:

Predict your emotional energy to optimize your professional experience.

Since he knew he would forget things and it would drive him crazy, and he knew he wasn't dealing with the phone calls adequately, he had to change his ways.

A notepad made a difference. A new outgoing voicemail made a difference. An answering service made a difference.

But the real change? New habits.

Learning to capture whatever thought came into his head on paper took dedication. Learning to transfer this to his spreadsheet each day took even more.

Jackson was able to take a longer view of his business. He was able to review his day, his week, and his ideas.

Stepping back gave him perspective.

Which is exactly what comes next.

Chapter 14

A Review of Everything

"If you change the way you look at things,
the things you look at change." –Wayne Dyer

THE FAMED BUSINESS GURU PETER DRUCKER once stated, "Time is the scarcest resource and unless it is managed nothing else can be managed."

And he's right. But he's also wrong.

We do need to take control of how we utilize time before we can do just about anything else. But "manage" is not the word we should use. And "time" isn't something that we can allocate and reallocate like a business professional deciding where to put their capital and where to assign their employees.

Instead, it's how we fill up the hours we have. And more importantly, it's how we *feel* about what we have to do with that time.

That starts with misconceptions. In Chapter 1 we covered the elements that impact our time in ways we don't often acknowledge or appreciate. Interruptions are when others pull us from whatever task we have at hand—usually because we allow them to. Distractions are other pieces of information in the environment or swimming around in our head. We look to these instead of what we know we should be doing.

Figuring out what we should be doing and how long it will take seems like a straightforward task. But we are inaccurate, mostly because of intrapersonal dynamics. After all, we don't want to miss the deadline, but we don't want others to think we padded the schedule.

And when we decide how long something should take, we tend to be imprecise. That is, we don't really break the work down into small enough pieces to have a good estimate.

When taken altogether, these factors can generate social tension. We can feel that our time is being wasted, or that we are annoying others with our bids for their time. We can feel that our time is too valuable for some work. Or, we can sense that others think we're asking them for something not worthy of them.

Our emotions are powerful predictors of what will happen with our time. Being aware of how we feel, and choosing how we react (to the extent it is possible) may be the most important time management lesson of all.

Chapter 2 is a crash course on this idea. Emotional energy is real, and is what psychologists call *positive affective arousal*. The scientific evidence is clear: when you feel good about what you just did, what you are now doing, and what comes next, you'll get more done overall.

Which is why the mantra of the book is, once again:

> **Predict your emotional energy to optimize your professional experience.**

If you know how you're going to feel before you have the feeling, you can plan accordingly. Of course, it's not perfect. Of course, life is not completely predictable.

But if you have some clue, you've got an edge. Which is why Chapter 3 is all about the best and worst part of determining how we're going to feel: understanding other people.

We all have people we look forward to seeing and those we dread. People who lighten our load and people who give us more to do.

Asking questions about those interactions can help us to better engage with our lives. Do we need to allocate time to prepare? What is likely to be discussed at the meeting? Will it start or end on time?

Every conversation with another person might be best associated with one of three feelings: appreciated, anxious, or angry. Having a sense of how you might feel can give you better insight on how to structure your schedule.

And if you know how people will make you feel, it's time to turn to tasks—the subject of Chapter 4.

Most of us are so busy with minutiae that we don't ever take time to think broadly about all of the commitments and opportunities in our life. That's why it can be intimidating to take out a blank piece of paper and write down the entirety of our task list.

And yet, in the business of time management the inventory of what we want and need to do is the most valuable asset we have. Like the superstore down the street, it's all the stuff on the shelves that comprise the vast majority of the investment. And like your own tasks, anything that sits too long may spoil.

But just like every product for sale is a different size and shape, sells for a specific price, and has an expiration date, every task on your list needs to be treated uniquely.

Knocking out a project may give you a sense of **relief** that it's finally done or leave with you **regret** that you've been avoiding feeling.

And that next item on your list may be something you merely **desire** the opportunity to work on, or strongly **dislike** even thinking about.

Your projects might be things that only you can do and **own**. Or, they could be delegated—**outsourced**—to someone else.

The work could be something **simple** that doesn't require much thinking or training. Or it might be a task that takes a high level of **skill** to complete.

And finally, a task might be **casual**: easy to complete in the background without much attention. Or it could be **challenging** where you need to focus your concentration to get it done right.

Scoring your tasks using these positive and negative criteria is one step of conquering your tasks. But conquering them by doing them is another.

Momentum is powerful. It keeps satellites orbiting the planet without the need for constant boost.

But that initial boost sometimes takes more energy than we can imagine. The start is often the hardest part.

In fact, reflecting on what you've already done today may be the best way to give yourself the motivation to do something more. Because getting something done every day helps ensure you get something done tomorrow.

The question, then, is what to do next?

Any serious investigation into time management will involve developing a process for organizing the items you need to do. Like the workers deep in the bowels of the post office, you need your very own sorting machine to route your tasks.

It's natural to want this to be a ready-to-go, off-the-shelf solution that works for anybody. But each of us is an individual with distinctive needs. We have to build our own system that lets us manage our work in the way that makes the most sense.

Your own machine has two fundamental elements: **dimensions** and **stages**. A dimension is a location where tasks reside: your email inbox, that pile of papers where you dump the mail, or the whiteboard on your desk. A stage is one of three steps in the process of completing a task: understanding the inputs, developing and following an action plan, and then moving the task to a queue to get completed.

It's not easy to build or to use. And operating your own task sorting machine requires combining all the lessons you've learned.

It means not just knowing you need to have a system, but writing it out and drawing its parts and pieces.

And it means understanding what to do—and what not to do—when managing your time.

It's these fundamental questions of best and worst practices that end the book. Chapter 9 lists them one at a time: what you should try and what you should avoid. And Chapters 10 through 14 bring together stories of people who learned to change how they managed their time (and the people around them) by changing their behavior.

Whether it's the tips from Chapter 9 or the stories from the pages that follow, or it's the systems that build up principles in the previous chapter, the thesis stays the same:

> **Predict your emotional energy to optimize your professional experience.**

You know how you're going to feel when it comes to most of the things you need to do.

Take advantage of that knowledge. Be aware of what emotions are headed your way. Acknowledge the complexity of your tasks. Decide who and what will energize you or drain you.

Figure out what you need to do yourself and what you can delegate away.

Because this is your life, and your chance to get things done.

And once what you have to do today is no longer hanging over your head, the rest of the day is yours.

Once the work for the week is complete, the fun for the week beings.

Because the more efficient we can be, the more happiness we can have: through the thrill of accomplishment and through the relaxation of choosing to accomplish nothing.

Take your time.

Take your time *back*.

It was always yours, and can be yours again.

Appendix

A Basis in Science

"Science and everyday life cannot and should not be separated." –Rosalind Franklin

PSYCHOLOGY IS DEFINED AS THE SCIENTIFIC STUDY of behavior and mental processes. Human beings have been interested in the way we think and act back to ancient times. Up until the 19th century, however, there was no rigorous academic work being done to try to understand the way our minds operate. Instead, these questions were left to philosophers and religious scholars.

For the majority of the 20th century and in the eyes of the public, the field of psychology was focused on understanding thought and behavior through a variety of psychoanalytic techniques. Ask the average person on the street and they would tell you psychologists studied feelings. They would also say that many of their patients were unstable or insane.

In reality, however, researchers were quietly developing a vast library of complex models based on real-world experiments. In 1948, for example, Bertram R. Forer gave a group of his students a new personality test he had devised. After tabulating the results, each participant would get a brief description of their distinct typology. Forer asked them to judge the accuracy of the assessments on a scale of 0 (very poor) to 5 (excellent). The average score was 4.26. The professor than revealed that the students—all thirty-nine of them—had received exactly the same brief description of their personality.

This phenomenon is now called the Forer Effect. It is our tendency to accept descriptions of our personality as long as we believe they were crafted specifically for us. Further experiments have refined and extended the idea, and shown situations in which it is more pronounced and less effective.

Simply *knowing* about the Forer Effect can reduce the chances you'll fall victim to a charlatan trying to take your money. But also, it can give you increased confidence when you do come across a legitimate mechanism for understanding yourself better: whether it's a personality test or some other psychological finding.

Tens of thousands of scientific studies have been done, and some offer profound insight into how we think and feel. Some effects are stronger than others. Some are directly applicable to time management, while others only provide hints as to why we are the way we are.

The critical work of understanding what we do and why we do it, however, is far from complete. In 2015, a large group of researchers published the results of the Reproducibility Project. They repeated a hundred different famous psychology experiments—but were only able to show their predicted outcomes about a third of the time.

Such challenges have not discouraged psychologists. Instead, they continue to look for mechanisms to explain human behavior and thinking processes, and they especially try to seek out connections between different ideas. Likewise in this appendix findings are cross-referenced to each other where applicable, but to see how they might be used to improve how you manage your time, refer back to the main part of the book.

New findings in social and industrial psychology are announced on daily basis. To stay current, follow current events in the press or visit the companion website to the book at www.efficientprofessional.com.

Enjoy!

Anchoring Effect [AE]: When gathering data, the first piece of information we learn usually gets more weight than it truly deserves.

Like a ship pulling into harbor, the anchor tends to fix us in a particular place and makes it harder to move somewhere else. If a salesperson gives an initial price, that number is anchored in our mind. Subsequent prices that are lower will seem especially attractive when compared with the first price. But in reality, the first price could have been much too high to begin with, so the lower offers only seem good in comparison.

The first piece of data—the anchor—can lead us astray. Be aware.

See also Endowment Effect [EE], Functional Fixedness [FF]

Mussweiler, T., Strack, F., & Pfeiffer, T. (2000). Overcoming the inevitable anchoring effect: Considering the opposite compensates for selective accessibility. *Personality and Social Psychology Bulletin, 26*(9), 1142-1150.

Strack, F., & Mussweiler, T. (1997). Explaining the enigmatic anchoring effect: Mechanisms of selective accessibility. *Journal of Personality and Social Psychology*, 73(3), 437.

Attribution Theory [AT]: We tend to behavior as being entirely caused by personality or situations.

Human conduct is complex. Yet research shows that when it comes to people besides ourselves, we usually decide what they do is either dispositional or situational. We say things like "that's just the way they are" or "that's the kind of person she is" to rationalize someone's behavior as being part of their personality. Or, we claim that "they are going through a lot right now" or "they just got lucky."

Because of this simplification, we often make mistakes when explaining our own behavior or that of others. These perceptions impact our estimates about the emotional impact of tasks as well as the time required to complete them.

See also Fundamental Attribution Error [FAE], Illusory Superiority [IS], Learned Helplessness [LH]

Harvey, P., & Dasborough, M. T. (2006). Consequences of employee attributions in the workplace: The role of emotional intelligence. *Psicothema*, 18.

Malle, B. F. (2011). Attribution theories: How people make sense of behavior. *Theories in Social Psychology, 23*, 72-95.

Buffering Effect [BFE]: The impact of stressors depends largely on our self-concept and our relationship with friends and family.

Research shows that the more we think of our own competency and the more people we think we can rely on, the better we are at dealing with stress. These factors create a "buffer" to negative experiences and reduces their impact. Even if we don't actually speak with close associates about the challenges in our life, evidence indicates that because we know they are there, we feel more comfortable dealing with stress.

The buffering effect also manifests when we are working in areas where we overestimate our expertise. Surprisingly, however, it does not seem to be connected to self-esteem. Awareness of this phenomenon can help individual planning and can provide guidance to management about encouraging team members to have active social connections outside of work.

See also Dunning-Krueger Effect [DKE]

Cummins, R. C. (1990). Job stress and the buffering effect of supervisory support. *Group & Organization Studies, 15*(1), 92-104.

Harrod, M. M. (2013). Further Examining the Buffering Effect of Self-Esteem and Mastery on Emotions. *Current Research in Social Psychology, 21.* 42-51.

Bandwagon Effect [BWE]: If we learn something is popular, we are more likely to embrace it.

Our decisions should be based only on the available facts. But when we have information about the popularity of an idea, a product, or a service, we tend to give the opinions of others significant weight. This can happen even if we don't personally know those people, or if we can't be certain they are truly real such as with online reviews.

In some cases, the majority opinion can cause us to choose answers we know to be false. This was famously demonstrated in the Asch conformity studies, where groups of participants were asked to answer simple questions such as which was the longer of two lines. Because there were confederates in the study who insisted on supporting a wrong answer, many people capitulated even though they knew better.

The effect causes us to feel protected by associating ourselves with the majority. A version of this phenomenon is captured by the expression "No one ever got fired for buying from the #1 vendor." That is, we feel safer in making choices we perceive as popular. To counter the effect, be conscious of the weight of opinions over facts.

See also Social Desirability Bias [SDB]

Asch, S. E., & Guetzkow, H. (1951). Effects of group pressure upon the modification and distortion of judgments. *Documents of Gestalt Psychology*, 222-236.

Leibenstein, H. (1950). Bandwagon, snob, and Veblen effects in the theory of consumers' demand. *The Quarterly Journal of Economics, 64*(2), 183-207.

Mehrabian, L. (1998). Effects of poll reports on voter preferences. *Journal of Applied Social Psychology, 28*(23), 2119-2130..

Bystander Effect [BYE]: When multiple people are confronted with a crisis, they become paralyzed and tend toward inaction. The more people there are, the less likely any one person is to try and help.

This phenomenon was first discovered following the 1964 murder of Kitty Genovese, in which it was reported that several dozen people witnessed the attacks but did not act until well after she was killed and the perpetrator had fled. Although the details of this story have since been disputed, studies have shown that people in a group are hesitant to take action as they assume the others will do so.

The bystander effect has some of the strongest empirical support of any concept in social psychology. In short, everyone thinks somebody else is going to do something, so nobody does.

Surprisingly, more recent studies show when there are negative consequences for the person who decides to step up and help, bystanders are more likely to assist.

See also Cognitive Dissonance [CD], Social Loafing [SCL]

Fischer, P., & Greitemeyer, T. (2013). The positive bystander effect: Passive bystanders increase helping in situations with high expected negative consequences for the helper. *The Journal of Social Psychology, 153*(1), 1-5.

Manning, R., Levine, M., & Collins, A. (2007). The Kitty Genovese murder and the social psychology of helping: The parable of the 38 witnesses. *American Psychologist, 62*(6), 555.

Choice Blindness [CB]: Our devotion to justifying a choice is often greater than our commitment to making that choice in the first place.

Imagine you're at a grocery store, and two varieties of jam are presented for you to try. You pick your favorite, and then a few minutes later are given an additional sample of your preferred selection and asked to justify your choice. Would you notice if they secretly gave you the flavor you *didn't* select?

Multiple studies have shown that upwards of 80% of participants do not realize they were given an item they did not choose and proceeded to explain why it was superior. This is the phenomenon of choice blindness. We are better at rationalizing what we selected than we are at remembering it. Accordingly, when planning our work and our schedule, we are less likely to be flexible once we are committed.

See also Ego Depletion [EGO]

Hall, L., Johansson, P., Tärning, B., Sikström, S., & Deutgen, T. (2010). Magic at the marketplace: Choice blindness for the taste of jam and the smell of tea. *Cognition, 117*(1), 54-61.

Taya, F., Gupta, S., Farber, I., & O'Dhaniel, A. (2014). Manipulation detection and preference alterations in a choice blindness paradigm. *PloS One, 9*(9), e108515.

Classical Conditioning [CC]: We can develop a response to a stimulus even if there is no valid reason for the response.

One of the most well-known phenomena in psychology, classical conditioning was first documented by Ivan Pavlov at the end of the 19th century. The original example of a natural stimulus-response—presenting food to a dog makes them salivate—can be associated with another stimulus at the same time—like ringing a bell. By repeating this process, you can eventually make a dog salivate merely by ringing the bell.

Because conditioning is a fundamental neural process, we can even use it on ourselves to change our behavior. This is sometimes called *self-consequation* as we are creating consequences to our own actions. We can even do it to some degree through merely *imagining* the conditioning. We can also use this effect as a mechanism to improve our memory, especially if we use associations with real-world objects to create reminders instead of electronic ones.

See also Dual Process Theory [DPT]

Baccus, J. R., Baldwin, M. W., & Packer, D. J. (2004). Increasing implicit self-esteem through classical conditioning. *Psychological Science, 15*(7), 498-502.

Hayes, S., et al. (1985). Self-reinforcement effects: an artifact of social standard setting? *Journal of Applied Behavior Analysis. 18*(3), 201-284.

Morewedge, C. K., Huh, Y. E., & Vosgerau, J. (2010). Thought for food: Imagined consumption reduces actual consumption. *Science, 330*(6010), 1530-1533.

Papini, M. R., & Bitterman, M. E. (1990). The role of contingency in classical conditioning. *Psychological Review*, 97(3), 396-403.

Rogers, T., & Milkman, K. L. (2016). Reminders Through Association. *Psychological Science, 27*(7), 973–986.

Cognitive Dissonance [CD]: The mental stress we experience when we hold multiple contradictory views at the same time.

A recurring theme throughout the history of psychology is that human beings want internal consistency in the way they see the world. There are many paradigms within cognitive dissonance theory, but all of them have one framework in common: that when challenged, people will expend considerable effort to keep an existing belief.

Modern neuroscience has provided confirmation for this phenomenon, and researchers have found applications from consumer behavior to politics to education. In time management, establishing recurring structures can help create comfort. Identifying areas where actions or thoughts are in contrast can lead to better resource management.

See also Decoy Effect [DCE], Mindfulness [MFL]

Festinger, L. (1957). A theory of cognitive dissonance (Vol. 2). Stanford University Press.

Van Veen, V., Krug, M. K., Schooler, J. W., & Carter, C. S. (2009). Neural activity predicts attitude change in cognitive dissonance. *Nature Neuroscience, 12*(11), 1469.

Cognitive Fixation [CF]: We often feel the only way to concentrate is to shut out distractions, but we are better at being creative when doing something else at the same time.

Evidence shows that multitasking reduces efficiency and accuracy in technical work. However, creative problem solving benefits from routine, low-cognition activities. This may explain why we frequently have ideas when showering, doing dishes, or completing other mundane tasks.

See also Dual Process Theory [DPT], Flow [FL], Mindfulness [MFL]

Lu, Jackson & Akinola, Modupe & Mason, Malia. (2017). "Switching On" creativity: Task switching can increase creativity by reducing cognitive fixation. Organizational Behavior and Human Decision Processes. 139. 63-75. 10.1016/j.obhdp.2017.01.005.

Chronotype Theory [CT]: Rather than "morning persons" and "night owls" researchers identify at least four types who have different schedules where they work best.

Extensive, long term studies have revealed several major groups. These include "dolphins" who tend to be light sleepers who often have insomnia; "lions" who wake up with lots of energy but are exhausted by early evening;

"bears" whose internal clocks match the sun, and "wolves" who have difficulty waking early but are most energetic at night.

Research shows that self-awareness of chronotype and discussion of schedules among teams can improve productivity and happiness.

See also Sleep-Enhanced Learning [SEL]

Facer-Childs, E.R., Bolling, S., & Balanos G.M. (2018). The effects of time of day and chronotype on cognitive and physical performance in healthy volunteers. *Sports Medicine-Open.* 4(1). 47.

Roenneberg, T., Wirz-Justice, A., & Merrow, M. (2003). Life between Clocks: Daily Temporal Patterns of Human Chronotypes. *Journal of Biological Rhythms, 18*(1), 80-90.

Volk, S., Pearsall, M. J., Christian, M. S., & Becker, W. J. (2017). Chronotype diversity in teams: Toward a theory of team energetic asynchrony. *Academy of Management Review, 42*(4), 683-702.

Decoy Effect [DCE]: New, inauthentic options can influence decision making.

Suppose a local newspaper offers their online-only subscription for $50 a year, and the online plus print edition for $100 a year. Given these two choices, some people will choose the online-only and others will choose the combo package.

But if they add a print-only option for $90 a year, then people are *more* likely to choose the $100 print-plus-online version. The print-only choice acts as a decoy.

This effect works in more than just consumer pricing. It can influence how often we wash our hands or engage in other desired behaviors. The decoy makes the more costly choice seem especially attractive, but only if that decoy is truly a bad option. Researchers call this *asymmetric dominance* because the deceptive choice must be out of sync with the previously existing choices.

When planning our time, coordinating with others, or presenting options to a team, the effect can be used to sway behavior.

See also Endowment Effect [EE], Priming [PRI]

Huber, J., Payne, J. W., & Puto, C. (1982). Adding asymmetrically dominated alternatives: Violations of regularity and the similarity hypothesis. *Journal of Consumer Research, 9*(1), 90-98.

Li, M., Sun, Y., & Chen, H. (2019). The decoy effect as a nudge: boosting hand hygiene with a worse option. *Psychological Science, 30*(1), 139-149.

Delayed Gratification [DG]: The ability to resist temptation now in exchange for a reward that is coming later.

We all want to relax. We want to eat the candy bar, watch a television show, or spend time doing anything other than working. Our ability to consciously delay doing something "fun" is part of self-control, which requires work.

In a classic delayed gratification experiment, young children are offered a single marshmallow and promised they will get a second one if they can hold off on eating it while the experimenter leaves the room. Some of the participants consume the first marshmallow immediately; others are able to resist for a few minutes before giving in. The rest are patient and receive their prize of two marshmallows in total.

Research shows that the ability to wait to eat the second marshmallow as a child correlates with academic and professional success, healthy eating and exercise habits. Studies have also demonstrated using the effect to address attention-seeking behavior in others, such as in a classroom environment.

See also Ego Depletion [EGO]

Austin, J. L., & Bevan, D. (2011). Using differential reinforcement of low rates to reduce children's requests for teacher attention. *Journal of Applied Behavior Analysis, 44*(3), 451-461.

Casey, B. J., Somerville, L. H., Gotlib, I. H., Ayduk, O., Franklin, N. T., Askren, M. K., ... & Glover, G. (2011). Behavioral and neural correlates of delay of gratification 40 years later. *Proceedings of the National Academy of Sciences, 108*(36), 14998-15003.

Mischel, W., & Ebbesen, E. B. (1970). Attention in delay of gratification. *Journal of Personality and Social Psychology, 16*(2), 329.

Dunning-Kruger Effect [DKE]: Novices overestimate their ability; true experts minimize their ability because they are aware of their own limitations.

The adage is true: we don't know what we don't know. Yet, when participants are asked to score their own ability in a particular field they tend to rank themselves too generously. This overconfidence leads to poor decision-making and misplaced blame for errors.

See also Earned Dogmatism [EDG], Group Think [GT]

Kruger, J., & Dunning, D. (1999). Unskilled and unaware of it: how difficulties in recognizing one's own incompetence lead to inflated self-assessments. *Journal of Personality and Social Psychology, 77*(6), 1121.

Pennycook, G., Ross, R. M., Koehler, D. J., & Fugelsang, J. A. (2017). Dunning–Kruger effects in reasoning: Theoretical implications of the failure to recognize incompetence. *Psychonomic Bulletin & Review, 24*(6), 1774-1784.

Dual Process Theory [DPT]: When encountering information our brains tend to choose either the automatic path or the conscious path based on how much cognitive work we think the data will require.

This is an enormous area of research in psychology, sociology, education, and economics. Dual process theory says that we have an unconscious pathway (system 1) and an intentional one (system 2). The latter appears to be unique to humans.

As we gain practice with activities, there is some evidence they can shift from system 2 to system 1 and require less conscious thought. The theory has been reinforced by neurological studies and real-world experiments. A critical element of individual productivity is the transition of tasks between systems. This includes doing routine work more automatically, and identifying when to switch to system 2 to address errors, problems, and exceptions.

See also Classical Conditioning [CC], Cognitive Fixation [CF], Flow [FL]

Goel, V., & Dolan, R. J. (2003). Explaining modulation of reasoning by belief. *Cognition, 87*(1), B11-B22.

Groves, P. M., & Thompson, R. F. (1970). Habituation: a dual-process theory. *Psychological Review, 77*(5), 419.

Doorway Effect [DWE]: When we walk into a new room, we sometimes forget the reason we went into it in the first place.

Changing our location can cause a decline in short term memory according to new research. This is because of at least two factors: information in our brains is encoded to match the context where it is needed (the room we started in) and information tends to get pushed out as we subconsciously predict it is no longer required.

The doorway effect seems to happen in virtual as well as physical spaces, so being taken away from your computer screen can cause you to lose your place as well. To prevent this from occurring, bring physical reminders or recite a key fact to keep it in short term memory.

See also Miller's Law [ML], Rehearsal Effect [RHE], Ziergarnick Effect [ZE]

Radvansky, G. A., Krawietz, S. A., & Tamplin, A. K. (2011). Walking through doorways causes forgetting: Further explorations. *The Quarterly Journal of Experimental Psychology, 64*(8), 1632-1645.

Witt, J. K. (2011). Action's effect on perception. *Current Directions in Psychological Science, 20*(3), 201-206.

Earned Dogmatism [EDG]: The more you perceive yourself as an expert the more you are likely to be closed to new ideas.

When people hold the title of "expert" they tend to become more rigid and closed-minded. The effect can occur even when individuals are only given the title temporarily. Simply being aware of the false confidence supplied by the label "expert" can help reduce the power of this effect.

See also Dunning-Kruger Effect [DKE], Earned Dogmatism [EDG], Group Think [GT]

Ottati, V., Price, E. D., Wilson, C., & Sumaktoyo, N. (2015). When self-perceptions of expertise increase closed-minded cognition: The earned dogmatism effect. *Journal of Experimental Social Psychology, 61*, 131-138.

Emotional Contagion [EC]: Emotions can spread like a disease from person to person and can even be transmitted through phone calls or email.

Although we often perceive emotions as individual experiences, they are collectively defined in societies and expressed using social cues. Laboratory work supports this effect, showing a measurable demonstration of the power of being positive—or negative. Team productivity can be dramatically impacted by the feelings of one individual.

See also Priming [PRI]

Bartel, C. A., & Saavedra, R. (2000). The collective construction of work group moods. *Administrative Science Quarterly, 45*(2), 197-231.

Hatfield, E., Cacioppo, J. T., & Rapson, R. L. (1993). Emotional contagion. *Current Directions in Psychological Science*, 2(3), 96-100.

Kramer, A. D., Guillory, J. E., & Hancock, J. T. (2014). Experimental evidence of massive-scale emotional contagion through social networks. *Proceedings of the National Academy of Sciences, 111*(24), 8788-8790.

Endowment Effect [EE]: We give greater value to something if we own it—even if we just got it.

First discovered in 1980 via collaboration between economists and psychologists, the effect is readily demonstrated in an experiment where participants are given a choice of a chocolate bar or a coffee mug. A large majority select the sweet. But when free mugs are distributed and people are given the chance to *trade* for chocolate, most want to keep their mugs.

Likewise, we give oversized weight to particular relationships, work responsibilities, or areas of expertise. Counteracting these can be challenging but doing so ultimately empowers us to be more productive.

See also Anchoring Effect [AE]

Beggan, J. K. (1992). On the social nature of nonsocial perception: The mere ownership effect. *Journal of Personality and Social Psychology, 62*(2), 229.

Kahneman, D., Knetsch, J. L., & Thaler, R. H. (1991). Anomalies: The endowment effect, loss aversion, and status quo bias. *Journal of Economic perspectives, 5*(1), 193-206.

Morewedge, C. K., Shu, L. L., Gilbert, D. T., & Wilson, T. D. (2009). Bad riddance or good rubbish? Ownership and not loss aversion causes the endowment effect. *Journal of Experimental Social Psychology, 45*(4), 947-951.

Pedersen, C. L. (2018). Managing the Distraction-Focus Paradox. *MIT Sloan Management Review, 59*(4), 72-+.

Ego Depletion [EGO]: Self-control is a limited resource that can be used up and needs to be replenished.

We're familiar with physical energy. Rest, food, and fluids are needed to work. Once our reserves expire, we need to recharge. Research shows that psychological energy works the same way, particularly with tasks requiring willpower. Multiple types of experiments demonstrate that if you force yourself to do something unpleasant (like ignoring a plate of oven-fresh cookies) you'll have a harder time later doing something intellectually challenging (like completing a crossword). This effect lingers even after the negative stimulus is removed.

Additional studies show that one technique for reducing the impact of ego depletion is to have a clear life purpose. Participants who self-identify as driven toward specific, large-scale goals tend to have greater willpower regardless of the unpleasant task at hand.

See also Delayed Gratification [DG], Rebound Effect [RBE]

Baumeister, R. F. (2002). Ego depletion and self-control failure: An energy model of the self's executive function. *Self and Identity, 1*(2), 129-136.

Garrison, K. E., Finley, A. J., & Schmeichel, B. J. (2018). Ego depletion reduces attention control: Evidence from two high-powered preregistered experiments. Personality and Social Psychology Bulletin, https://doi.org/10.1177/0146167218796473.

Fundamental Attribution Error [FAE]: The belief that others experience misfortune due to their flaws, but we experience misfortune due to circumstances beyond our control.

This concept highlights a key aspect of psychology: that we expect people to think and act like us but not to be as skilled as we are. Furthermore the effect happens in reverse. That is, we imagine our successes arise more often due to hard work yet others often succeed because of luck or because they cheated.

Recognizing that all people have a similar experience in this regard can increase empathy and promote collaboration among workplace teams.

See also Dunning-Kruger Effect [DKE], False Consensus Effect [FCE], Illusion of Control [ICO], Illusory Correlation [ICR]

Ayoko, O. B. (2016). Workplace conflict and willingness to cooperate: The importance of apology and forgiveness. *International Journal of Conflict Management, 27*(2), 172-198.

Rogoff, E. G., Lee, M. S., & Suh, D. C. (2004). "Who done it?" Attributions by entrepreneurs and experts of the factors that cause and impede small business success. *Journal of Small Business Management, 42*(4), 364-376.

False Consensus Effect [FCE]: We believe others think the way we do, and furthermore, tend to have strong opinions about the personalities of people who don't.

Everyone is different, but every person lives inside their own head. We are biased to approve of our own thought processes, our own emotions, and our own reactions. We usually assume others will act similarly and are skeptical of those who don't. This creates conflict while ironically, diversity of views often benefits teams and enhances problem solving.

See also Fundamental Attribution Error [FAE], Self-verification Theory [SVT]

Bauman, K. P., & Geher, G. (2002). We think you agree: The detrimental impact of the false consensus effect on behavior. *Current Psychology, 21*(4), 293-318.

Marks, G., & Miller, N. (1987). Ten years of research on the false-consensus effect: An empirical and theoretical review. *Psychological Bulletin, 102*(1), 72-90.

Functional Fixedness [FF]: Once we know what an object is used for, that's what we think it will *always* be used for.

Also known as "the law of the instrument", this idea is often popularized with the expression "if all you have is a hammer, everything looks like a nail." In workplaces, technologies, systems, and social patterns tend to fall victim to functional fixedness. For example: when in doubt, have a meeting; when data needs to be tracked, create a spreadsheet. These tools may not be ideal for the task at hand, but they readily available and thus quickly employed.

See also Anchoring Effect [AE], Endowment Effect [EE], Schemata Theory [SCT]

Adamson, R. E. (1952). Functional fixedness as related to problem solving: A repetition of three experiments. *Journal of Experimental Psychology, 44*(4), 288.

McCaffrey, T. (2012). Innovation relies on the obscure: A key to overcoming the classic problem of functional fixedness. *Psychological Science, 23*(3), 215-218.

Flow [FL]: When we are working on tasks that are challenge us and require specialized skills, we can get into a mental concentrative state of maximum productivity that is highly sensitive to interruptions and distractions.

As a foundational element of the positive psychology movement, "flow" describes the pinnacle of human intellectual focus. Experiments show it can take participants in carefully-designed environments up to a half hour for the brain to enter this state. Distractions of only a few seconds in duration can end it.

Flow is also linked to high performance in a wide variety of fields, as well as persistence in achievement, reduction in anxiety, and a rise in self-esteem.

See also Dual-Process Theory [DPT], Cognitive Fixation [CF]

Csikszentmihalyi, M. (2014). Toward a psychology of optimal experience. In *Flow and the Foundations of Positive Psychology* (pp. 209-226). Springer, Dordrecht.

Robertson, I. T., Jansen Birch, A., & Cooper, C. L. (2012). Job and work attitudes, engagement and employee performance: where does psychological well-being fit in?. *Leadership & Organization Development Journal, 33*(3), 224-232.

Walker, C. J. (2010). Experiencing flow: Is doing it together better than doing it alone?. *The Journal of Positive Psychology, 5*(1), 3-11.

Framing [FR]: Restructuring statements as intentionally biased perspectives can often influence mood and thought patterns.

Which meat would you buy? The one labeled "80% lean" or another marked "20% fat?" Is that piece of clothing "old" or "vintage?" Are you approaching your "twilight years" or your "golden years?" Although each is effectively identical, the choice of words can drive feelings and beliefs.

Experimental studies demonstrate that framing also hampers evaluation skills. Participants shown the same video of a motor vehicle incident judged the drivers more harshly and estimated higher speeds when the prompt used the phrase "crashed" than when "contacted."

Likewise, professionals can frame effectively—even when engaging in self-talk—to guide outcomes. A meeting can be "only an hour" (instead of a "full hour"); work can be something that we "get to do" (instead of have to do"); additional resources can be "extra" (instead of "waste.")

See also Priming [PRI]

Mowen, M. M., & Mowen, J. C. (1986). An empirical examination of the biasing effects of framing on business decisions. *Decision Sciences, 17*(4), 596-602.

Passera, S., Smedlund, A., & Liinasuo, M. (2016). Exploring contract visualization: clarification and framing strategies to shape collaborative business relationships. *Journal of Strategic Contracting and Negotiation, 2*(1-2), 69-100.

Gratitude Effect [GE]: Reflecting on specific positive experiences in our day improves overall mood and productivity.

When asked to keep a brief journal focused on what they are grateful for, participants report multiple long term positive effects. These include improved mood, energy, and attitude.

Analysis indicates that gratitude may be unique as a positive emotion. This is unlike hope (which can trigger uncertainty) or nostalgia (which can trigger regret.) For gratitude journaling to be effective the items listed should be distinctive to the individual, non-repeating, and have impacted them recently.

See also Buffering Effect [BFE], Hawthorne Effect [HWE]

Emmons, R. A., & McCullough, M. E. (2003). Counting blessings versus burdens: An experimental investigation of gratitude and subjective well-being in daily life. *Journal of Personality and Social Psychology, 88*, 377-389.

Goal Systems Theory [GST]: Instead of a goal as a singular objective, goals should be envisioned as a network of links.

Studies show that when we set a goal and we recognize there are other steps we have to accomplish first, we tend to overlook those other steps and invest more resources in the goal itself. We feel good about this choice, but paradoxically it reduces the quality of our decision making and overall effectiveness.

Under the systems theory model, goals include vertical components (means that must be achieved to fulfill ends) and lateral components (multiple competing goals or means). Mapping out long-term objectives with this framework improves planning accuracy and rate of success.

See also Illusion of Control [ICO], Outcome vs. Process Orientation [OPO]

Bodmann, S., Hulleman, C. & Harackiewicz, J. (2008). Achievement Goal Systems: An Application of Goal Systems Theory to Achievement Goal Research. *International Review of Social Psychology. Vol 21*(1), 71-96.

Kruglanski, A. W., Shah, J. Y., Fishbach, A., & Friedman, R. (2018). A theory of goal systems. In *The Motivated Mind* (pp. 215-258). Routledge.

> **Groupthink [GT]**: When teams make decisions, they value harmony and often rationalize bad ideas.

Inspired by the George Orwell n22ovel *1984*, this phenomenon occurs most readily under three conditions: (1) members are highly cohesive and seek to maintain friendly relations, (2) structural faults in group design that inhibit checking for errors or searching for problems, as well as bias toward group leaders, and (3) situational contexts such as recent failures, time pressures, and external threats.

Groupthink can be mitigated by intentionally designing against these elements. This may include discouraging socialization, encouraging "devil's advocates," having leaders periodically skip group meetings, and buffering any external constraints that should not affect the decision. In short: brainstorming is best done individually; randomly selected groups should evaluate ideas.

See also Social Desirability Bias [SDB]

Baron, R. S. (2005). So right it's wrong: Groupthink and the ubiquitous nature of polarized group decision making. *Advances in Experimental Social Psychology, 37*(2), 219-253.

Eaton, J. (2001). Management communication: the threat of groupthink. *Corporate Communications: An International Journal, 6*(4), 183–192.

Janis, I. L. (1972). Victims of Groupthink: a Psychological Study of Foreign-Policy Decisions and Fiascoes. Boston: Houghton Mifflin. ISBN 0-395-14002-1.

> **Hawthorne Effect [HWE]**: When people know they are being observed they modify their behavior.

This term is named for a series of industrial efficiency studies done at the Hawthorne Works factories in the late 1920s where researchers anticipated specific environmental changes (such as light levels) would impact worker productivity. Later analysis concluded that the key variable was that mere novelty of being a research subject inclined participants to work harder.

Although modern psychological models have more nuanced explanations for human behavior in these settings, the original concept persists as a component of workforce management and employee engagement. This ranges from performance evaluation systems to office architecture. That is, we are likely to change our behavior if we believe we are being watched and possibly experimented on—often regardless of our opinion of leadership.

See also Buffering Effect [BFE], In-group Bias/Identity Theory [IBIT], Priming [PRI]

Laird, B. K., Bailey, C. D., & Hester, K. (2018). The effects of monitoring environment on problem-solving performance. *The Journal of Social Psychology, 158*(2), 215-219.

Gou, Z. (2017). Workplace design revolution: The inside-out urbanism. In *Design Innovations for Contemporary Interiors and Civic Art* (pp. 225-240). IGI Global.

Intentional Blindness Effect [IBE]: Closing your eyes improves memory recall, promotes efficient formation of new memories, and improves unconscious attentiveness.

Colloquially, people often state that the five senses exist in balance and without one the others grow stronger.

Laboratory studies show tentative support for this idea. For example, participants can more accurately describe a recently viewed image if they close their eyes. This is also why drivers who are looking for landmarks or dealing with adverse weather turn down the radio so they can "see better."

Conversely, attentive focus on other sensations reduces our ability to detect novelty. In an experiment organized by *The Washington Post*, a world-class concert violinist with a multi-million dollar instrument performed in a subway terminal. A thousand commuters streamed by and almost no one noticed. In complimentary experiments on the phenomenon of selective attention, people talking on cellphones are less likely to notice unusual road hazards, and individuals instructed to count the number of passes in a basketball practice rarely spot a man in gorilla suit walking through the court.

See also Framing [FR]

Molloy, K., Griffiths, T. D., Chait, M., & Lavie, N. (2015). Inattentional deafness: visual load leads to time-specific suppression of auditory evoked responses. *Journal of Neuroscience, 35*(49), 16046-16054.

Nash, R. A., Nash, A., Morris, A., & Smith, S. L. (2016). Does rapport-building boost the eyewitness eyeclosure effect in closed questioning?. *Legal and Criminological Psychology, 21*(2), 305-318.

Simons, D. J., & Chabris, C. F. (1999). Gorillas in our midst: Sustained inattentional blindness for dynamic events. *Perception, 28*(9), 1059-1074.

In-group Bias/Identity Theory [IBIT]: We tend to favor the ideas of people we perceive to be on our "team" even to our own detriment.

Humans organize themselves into cliques with an "in-group" of those we consider like us and an "out-group" for those who are different. We are biased toward new ideas that come from our group and establish an identity as being with our group. Further conflict appears as individuals associate with multiple groups and develop varying commitments accordingly.

Reminding individuals of their in-group/out-group status can trigger stereotype responses and reinforce patterns of discrimination. Organizations function best when groups are defined consciously and efforts are made to promote cross-functional relationships.

See also Groupthink [GT], Priming [PRI]

Hebl, M., Ruggs, E. R., Martinez, L. R., Trump-Steele, R., & Nittrouer, C. (2015). Understanding and reducing interpersonal discrimination in the workplace. *Handbook of Prejudice, Stereotyping, and Discrimination*, 387.

Morris, R. C. (2013). Identity salience and identity importance in identity theory. *Current Research in Social Psychology, 21*(8), 23-36.

Impulse Control [IC]: The ability to consciously subdue immediate desires in exchange for longer term goals.

All of us have impulses we must choose whether or not to fulfill. This includes eating a tasty morsel of food or buying a well-marketed product. Accepting the craving gives us satisfaction and denying it requires emotional energy.

Research indicates that while animals can be trained to employ impulse control, humans use rationalization techniques as well purposeful environment changes to try and avoid acting on whim. Sleep, mindfulness, and forethought all seem to improve our success at managing our urges.

See also Delayed Gratification [DG], Ego Depletion [EGO]

Coviello, D., Deserranno, E., Persico, N., & Sapienza, P. (2017). *Effect of Mood on Workplace Productivity*. Unpublished manuscript.

Mendelson, R., Mantz, T., & Guity, F. (2015). Quantitative analysis of emotional intelligence in the workplace. *Journal of International Business and Economics*. (15)3. 107-117.

Illusion of Control [ICO]: We believe we have more power over events and outcomes then we actually do, which serves as a coping mechanism.

Almost everything in the world is driven by forces beyond our control. Even the choices we believe we have are influenced by the options that are available. Yet, multiple studies show that people tend to overestimate everything from their physical strength, social skills, mental capacity, knowledge of the stock market, and ability to convince others of a point of view.

The illusion of control may be necessary for modern survival, however, because it grants people the necessary confidence to begin new endeavors or take on activities where the path ahead is unclear. Awareness of this effect can help drive more realistic projections in short term and long term planning.

See also Dunning-Kruger Effect [DKE], Kappa Effect/Tau Effect [KETE], Flow [FL]

Coughlin, D. (2017). The any person mindset: the illusion of control. *Effective Executive, 20*(4), 62-63.

Fenton-O'Creevy, M., Nicholson, N., Soane, E., & Willman, P. (2003). Trading on illusions: Unrealistic perceptions of control and trading performance. *Journal of Occupational and Organizational Psychology, 76*(1), 53-68.

Langer, E. J. (1975). The illusion of control. *Journal of Personality and Social Psychology, 32*(2), 311.

Illusory Correlation [ICR]: We often see connections and patterns that don't actually exist.

Although the ability to discover associations is often beneficial to human progress, individuals can become more readily convinced they exist with minimal prompting. This effect spans a wide range of well-known behavior, including self-aware superstitions (e.g. "when I wear my lucky shirt my team always wins") and also recognition and reinforcement of stereotypes.

Illusory correlation also explains many forms of gambling or prediction fallacies (e.g. "we've had red four times in a row on the roulette wheel, so black *has* to come up next.") The effect can be reduced by consciously attempting to depersonalize and generalize experiences when we believe there is a connection.

See also Fundamental Attribution Error [FAE]

Aberizk, K., Newman, L. S., & Sargent, R. H. (2017). Attributional Complexity and the Illusory Correlation: A Test of the Inverted-U Hypothesis. *North American Journal of Psychology, 19*(3).

Hamilton, D. L., & Gifford, R. K. (1976). Illusory correlation in interpersonal perception: A cognitive basis of stereotypic judgments. *Journal of Experimental Social Psychology, 12*(4), 392-407.

Inaction Effect [IE]: Decisions to act produce more regret than decisions not to act. Therefore, choosing inaction often seems preferable.

We usually have two options: do something, or do nothing. The advantage to taking action is sense of control, but the drawback is the risk of failure and blame. If we take no action we avoid responsibility. While both paths are weighed at the time of the decision, our retrospective memory tends to hold greater self-disappointment regarding active choices over passive ones.

This phenomenon can lead to a preference for inaction and can contribute to so-called "analysis paralysis."

See also Illusion of Control [ICO]

Zeelenberg M., van de Bos. K, van Dijk E, Pieters R. (2002). The inaction effect in the psychology of regret. *Journal of Personality and Social Psychology, 82*(3), 314-327.

Itzkin, A., Van Dijk, D., & Azar, O. H. (2016). At least I tried: The relationship between regulatory focus and regret following action vs. inaction. *Frontiers in Psychology, 7*, 1684..

Illusory Superiority [IS]: A large majority of people believe they are above average—which is mathematically impossible.

Survey people about their driving skills, their charitable giving, their general knowledge, or their social awareness and more than half will claim they are better than the typical person. Since this is not possible, it will often lead individuals to take risks or make statements that are beyond their capacity.

Overestimates of ability have a significant micro effect on individual time management and lead to macro effects in large projects.

See also Dunning-Kruger Effect [DKE], Illusion of Control [ICO]

Dunning, D., Meyerowitz, J. A., & Holzberg, A. D. (1989). Ambiguity and self-evaluation: The role of idiosyncratic trait definitions in self-serving assessments of ability. *Journal of Personality and Social Psychology, 57*(6), 1082.

McCormick, I. A., Walkey, F. H., & Green, D. E. (1986). Comparative perceptions of driver ability—a confirmation and expansion. *Accident Analysis & Prevention, 18*(3), 205-208.

Kappa Effect/Tau Effect [KETE]: Our ability to estimate time is poor, especially when there is spatial or mental distance involved.

There are a large number of findings in modern psychology related to time perception. The *telescoping effect*, for example, is our tendency to recall recent events as occurring farther in the past and distant events as being more recent. The phenomenon known as *Vierordt's law* shows that shorter time intervals are often overestimated and longer time intervals are often underestimated. The term *chronostasis* refers to the effect shown by looking at the second hand of an analog clock, which will usually seem to be frozen at first glance.

All of these time perception errors may be related to a complementary pair of discoveries. The kappa effect appears when multiple stimuli are spaced at equal time intervals but across varying distances. Our brains are fooled by the spatial discrepancy into thinking the timing is not the same. The tau effect arises with equal distances, but varying times. Because the visual spacing is consistent, we misread the duration between each stimulus.

These biases may impact everything from estimation, memory, visual interpretation of schedules, and other aspects of time perception and management.

See also Illusion of Control [ICO], Illusory Superiority [IS]

Chen, Y., Zhang, B., & Kording, K. P. (2016). Speed constancy or only slowness: What drives the kappa effect. *PloS one, 11*(4), e0154013.

Suto, Y (1952). The effect of space on time estimation (S-effect) in tactual space (I). *Japanese Journal of Psychology, 22*: 45–57.

Learned Helplessness [LH]: When experiencing repeated discomfort without the possibility of relief, we sometimes believe escape is impossible even in other, unrelated situations.

Conceptual frameworks on individual agency often focus on the resources available to solve problems, reduce pain, or increase pleasure. In traditional studies involving animals or human participants in controlled environments, participants typically express distress after multiple failed attempts to improve their situation. This sensation can is associated with specific neurocircuitry and can remain with a subject long after the initial problem has vanished.

In workplaces, minor annoyances and patterns may be characterized as "we've always done it that way" and this thinking can spill over into areas that could be easily improved. Research indicates that learned helplessness can be reduced by major environmental changes as well as exercise.

See also Fundamental Attribution Error [FAE]

Greenwood, B. N., & Fleshner, M. (2008). Exercise, learned helplessness, and the stress-resistant brain. *Neuromolecular Medicine, 10*(2), 81-98.

Maier, S. F., & Seligman, M. E. (2016). Learned helplessness at fifty: Insights from neuroscience. *Psychological Review, 123*(4), 349.

Mental Contrasting [MC]: Instead of visualizing our dreams, we should imagine the obstacles to our goals and our techniques for overcoming them.

Self-help literature is filled with the supposed power of visualization. It is often erroneously claimed that basketball players who merely *imagine* completing perfect free throws improve their skill as effectively as if they had actually practiced.

However, visualization can be effective if used according to guidance from research studies. In particular, visualizing goals alone can be dangerous because it makes them seem easier than they actually are and can later result in feelings of inadequacy. Instead, imagining the process of steps involved can create a more realistic mental framework of the work ahead and improve the accuracy of planning.

See also Dunning-Kruger Effect [DKE], Goal Systems Theory [GST], Learned Helplessness [LH], Outcome vs. Process Orientation [OPO]

Oettingen, G., & Gollwitzer, P. M. (2017). Health behavior change by self-regulation of goal pursuit: Mental contrasting with implementation intentions. In *Routledge International Handbook of Self-Control in Health and Well-Being* (pp. 418-430). Routledge.

Oettingen, G., Kappes, H. B., Guttenberg, K. B., & Gollwitzer, P. M. (2015). Self-regulation of time management: Mental contrasting with implementation intentions. *European Journal of Social Psychology, 45*(2), 218-229.

Mindfulness [MFL]: Doing simple work consciously reduces stress and pain.

Metacognition (thinking about thinking) refers to the act of being aware of our thoughts and attempting to understand them. Mindfulness suggests intentionality about our actions—especially if those actions do not require much thought. This is believed to help shift our focus onto something we can control and give us a stronger sense of identity and purpose, even if only for a moment.

An enormous number of positive effects are associated with mindfulness, including weight loss, improved sleep, increased memory capacity and focus, as well reduction in painful sensations, stress, ruminations, and emotional reactivity.

See also Cognitive Fixation [CF], Flow [FL]

Black, D. S., O'Reilly, G. A., Olmstead, R., Breen, E. C., & Irwin, M. R. (2015). Mindfulness meditation and improvement in sleep quality and daytime impairment among older adults with sleep disturbances: a randomized clinical trial. *JAMA Internal Medicine, 175*(4), 494-501.

Hanley, A. W., Warner, A. R., Dehili, V. M., Canto, A. I., & Garland, E. L. (2015). Washing dishes to wash the dishes: brief instruction in an informal mindfulness practice. *Mindfulness, 6*(5), 1095-1103.

Loucks, E. B., Britton, W. B., Howe, C. J., Gutman, R., Gilman, S. E., Brewer, J., ... & Buka, S. L. (2016). Associations of dispositional mindfulness with obesity and central adiposity: the New England family study. *International Journal of Behavioral Medicine, 23*(2), 224-233.

Zeidan, F., Emerson, N. M., Farris, S. R., Ray, J. N., Jung, Y., McHaffie, J. G., & Coghill, R. C. (2015). Mindfulness meditation-based pain relief employs different neural mechanisms than placebo and sham mindfulness meditation-induced analgesia. *Journal of Neuroscience, 35*(46), 15307-15325.

Miller's Law [ML]: We are able to remember 7±2 pieces of information in short term memory.

One of the oldest and most celebrated areas of memory research, Miller's Law can easily be demonstrated by naming a series of items—such as single digits, common words, letters of the alphabet, or everyday objects—and asking a listener to repeat them back. People can typically recite a list of about seven items, or in some cases as few as five but rarely more than nine.

The key discovery associated with Miller's Law is that short-term memory is encoded as "chunks." We are great at remembering something for the next few seconds if it has a distinct and complete meaning. Individuals who want to better manage their time and communication in these short intervals should control the quantity of information they are attempting to remember with the 7±2 limit in mind.

See also Doorway Effect [DWE]

Cowan, N. (2010). The magical mystery four: How is working memory capacity limited, and why?. *Current Directions in Psychological Science, 19*(1), 51-57.

Miller, G. A. (1956). The magical number seven, plus or minus two: Some limits on our capacity for processing information. *Psychological Review, 63*(2), 81.

Moral Licensing [MOL]: Choosing an action we deem as "good" makes us feel justified in choosing a subsequent action that is not as good.

Whenever we are proud of a choice we just made—like being kind to a stranger, making it to the gym, or arriving early for an appointment—we become less critical of the downsides of doing something bad. This can even manifest in mere intentions. If you think "I'm going to start my new diet on Monday" you'll likely to rationalize having some chocolate cake today as "a reward."

In groups, the phenomenon can spread between persons. Effective interventions to stop moral licensing include reframing good work as its own reward, and separating moral choices from practical decisions.

See also Emotional Contagion [EC], In-Group Bias/Identity Theory [IBIT]

Kouchaki, M. (2011). Vicarious moral licensing: The influence of others' past moral actions on moral behavior. *Journal of Personality and Social Psychology, 101*(4), 702.

Mullen, E., & Monin, B. (2016). Consistency versus licensing effects of past moral behavior. *Annual Review of Psychology, 67*, 363-385.

Outcome Controllability [OC]: We credit positive outcomes to our own contributions, and rationalize negative outcomes as preventable if we had more control.

Counterfactual thinking is the psychological concept of asking "what if" about previous events. When reflecting on past experiences we unwittingly use counterfactuals to inflate our influence or explain what we would have done with more authority.

This reinforces a bias called outcome controllability that develops into such thoughts as "no one is working as hard as me," or "to do things right I have do them myself." Although these ideas serve as self-protection mechanisms, they also negatively impact group dynamics, social relationships, and the overall quality of work products.

See also Fundamental Attribution Error [FAE], Illusion of Control [ICO], Rehearsal Effect [RHE], Social loafing [SCL]

Baron, R. A. (2000). Counterfactual thinking and venture formation: The potential effects of thinking about "what might have been". *Journal of Business Venturing, 15*(1), 79-91.

Roese, N. J., & Olson, J. M. (Eds.). (2014). What might have been: The social psychology of counterfactual thinking. Psychology Press.

Outcome vs. Process Orientation [OPO]: We make better, smarter, and more satisfying decisions when we visualize the experience that would be created by our choice instead of the choice itself.

Decision-making in psychology is sometimes characterized by the central mental focus of the subject.

Although it requires additional time and mental energy, process-oriented thinking features several benefits when compared to outcome-oriented thinking. These include increased confidence and the self-adoption of decisiveness as trait. Process-oriented thinking is improved through role play and other interactive social techniques.

See also Goal Systems Theory [GST], Mental Contrasting [MC]

Leyer, M., Hirzel, A. K., & Moormann, J. (2018). Achieving sustainable behavioral changes of daily work practices: The effect of role plays on learning process-oriented behavior. *Business Process Management Journal,* 24(4), 1050-1068.

Thompson, D. V., Hamilton, R. W., & Petrova, P. K. (2009). When mental simulation hinders behavior: The effects of process-oriented thinking on decision difficulty and performance. *Journal of Consumer Research, 36*(4), 562-574.

Power Paradox [PP]: The skills that help people *gain* power tend to vanish once that power is attained.

Multiple studies have shown that we want people elevated to leadership roles when they demonstrate qualities such as the ability to listen and work with others, patience, and conflict resolution. But individuals in positions of authority are more likely to lack empathy and be impulsive.

In newly-formed groups, individuals who talk the most tend to be perceived as leaders, not those who are most knowledgeable or respectful. To address this paradox, leaders can actively focus on a servant mindset. Contributors can purposely thank leaders for inclusive behaviors.

See also Moral Licensing [MOL]

Anderson, C., & Kilduff, G. J. (2009). Why do dominant personalities attain influence in face-to-face groups? The competence-signaling effects of trait dominance. *Journal of Personality and Social Psychology, 96*(2), 491.

Sousa, M., & van Dierendonck, D. (2017). Servant leadership and the effect of the interaction between humility, action, and hierarchical power on follower engagement. *Journal of Business Ethics, 141*(1), 13-25.

de Vries, R. E., Pathak, R. D., & Paquin, A. R. (2011). The paradox of power sharing: Participative charismatic leaders have subordinates with more instead of less need for leadership. *European Journal of Work and Organizational Psychology, 20*(6), 779-804.

Priming [PRI]: Environmental information that may seem irrelevant to a task can influence orientation and mindset.

One of the more well-established aspects of social psychology, priming is demonstrated by a wide variety of experiments. In one study, participants that read essays related to "old age" later walked more slowly than those who did not. In another, individuals wearing a heavy backpack judged an image of hill as steeper than those who were unencumbered. One more test had people hold the experimenter's coffee cup for a few seconds while papers were shuffled, then presented. Their subsequent opinions correlated to the temperature of the beverage.

Priming can be used to influence others as well as ourselves. A clean desk, fresh smells, and even positive intentions often prime specific responses over others.

See also Emotional Contagion [EC], Framing [FR], Hawthorne Effect [HWE]

Pfeffer, J., & DeVoe, S. E. (2012). The economic evaluation of time: Organizational causes and individual consequences. *Research in Organizational Behavior, 32*, 47-62.

Weingarten, E., Chen, Q., McAdams, M., Yi, J., Hepler, J., & Albarracín, D. (2016). From primed concepts to action: A meta-analysis of the behavioral effects of incidentally presented words. *Psychological Bulletin, 142*(5), 472.

Personality Type Theories [PTT]: A wide variety of instruments designed to classify individuals into psychological categories with common attributes.

First popularized by the Greek physician Hippocrates, countless versions of personality "types" have been introduced. These range from Carl Jung's four factors, the Myers-Briggs Personality Type Indicator, the Enneagram, and Type A/Type B theory. In addition, the medical specialty of psychiatry has established criteria for disease-oriented personality disorders.

Modern research indicates that people do not conform to types but rather tend to cluster around specific traits. The most successful empirical system, the Five Factor model, characterizes individuals as having positive or negative scores on the axes of openness, conscientiousness, extraversion, agreeability, and neuroticism.

The primary benefit of personality type and trait theories may be to increase self-awareness as well as promote an interest in the development of others.

See also Framing, [FR] Hawthorne Effect [HWE], Priming [PRI]

Digman, J. M. (1990). Personality structure: Emergence of the five-factor model. *Annual Review of Psychology, 41*(1), 417-440.

Engler, B. (2-13). Personality theories: An introduction (9th ed.). Boston, MA, US: Houghton, Mifflin and Company.

Rebound Effect [RBE]: The more you try not to think about something or experience an emotion, the more likely it is to come back and haunt you.

Suppressing a thought is surprisingly difficult. We end up thinking about something else instead, and usually whatever we are avoiding "rebounds" back into our minds. In one study, the participants who were asked to *not* think about chocolate were those that ate the most.

This also impacts out ability to control bias. When we try to withhold judgment, we are actually more likely to be judgmental. Instead of avoidant patterns, individuals are more successful when making active choices.

See also Cognitive Fixation [CF], Ego Depletion [EGO]

Erskine, J. A., & Georgiou, G. J. (2013). Behavioral, cognitive, and affective consequences of trying to avoid chocolate. In *Chocolate in Health and Nutrition* (pp. 479-489). Humana Press, Totowa, NJ.

Yap, A. J., & Tong, E. M. (2009). The appraisal rebound effect: Cognitive appraisals on the rebound. *Personality and Social Psychology Bulletin, 35*(9), 1208-1219.

Rehearsal Effect [RHE]: We retain experiences more effectively if we spend time describing them.

Brain experts classify the ways we intentionally remember information into two categories. Type I, called *maintenance rehearsal,* is simply repeating or replaying the data multiple times without thinking about it. This is highly effective for keeping something in short term memory.

Type II, known as *elaborative rehearsal*, involves thinking about the meaning of material or creating other mental associations. This technique requires more effort and time, but has far greater results for long term memory.

The difference between Type I and Type II strategies and their relative efficacy is the core of the effect.

See also Ego Depletion [EGO], Miller's Law [ML]

Evans, J. D. (1974). The lag effect in free recall: differential encoding or differential rehearsal? *Retrospective Theses and Dissertations.* 6336.

Logan, J. M., Castel, A. D., Haber, S., & Viehman, E. J. (2012). Metacognition and the spacing effect: the role of repetition, feedback, and instruction on judgments of learning for massed and spaced rehearsal. *Metacognition and Learning, 7*(3), 175-195.

Social Loafing [SCL]: The larger a group working on a project, the less effort individuals in that group tend to contribute.

In a shared activity, it's usually impossible for all parties to contribute equally. However, because we tend to have low expectations of others and because large teams result in anonymity, we are more likely to be passive participants. This leads to reduced commitment and poorer results.

Effective methods for combating social loafing include organizing teams into smaller groups and delegating work to individuals wherever possible.

See also Bystander Effect [BYE], Illusory Superiority [IS], Moral Licensing [MOL], Outcome Controllability [OC]

Meyer, B., Schermuly, C. C., & Kauffeld, S. (2016). That's not my place: The interacting effects of faultlines, subgroup size, and social competence on social loafing behaviour in work groups. *European Journal of Work and Organizational Psychology, 25*(1), 31-49.

Singh, S., Zhu, M., & Wang, H. (2018). Effect of conflict and emotions on perceptions of social loafing in groups. *International Journal of Services, Economics and Management, 9*(1), 77-94.

Schemata Theory [SCT]: People develop cognitive structures to organize knowledge and guide information processing.

Although we are often not aware of it, when we begin learning about a new field we create a mental map of concepts that is filled in over time. Since most learning is informal, this process results in an inaccurate, but ever-changing framework.

As we progress, this *schema* takes the form of generalized beliefs that operate automatically and lead to biases in perception and memory (e.g. "yogurt is healthier than ice cream.") This makes it easier to work because we are following a system rather than answering each question individually.

Effective training techniques typically employ schema design throughout. Once major pathways in schemas are established, they are difficult to change even if proven to be incorrect.

See also Choice Blindness [CB], Dual Process Theory [DPT], Functional Fixedness [FF]

Martin, J. (1984). Toward a cognitive schemata theory of self-instruction. *Instructional Science, 13*(2), 159-180.

Martins, L. L., Rindova, V. P., & Greenbaum, B. E. (2015). Unlocking the hidden value of concepts: a cognitive approach to business model innovation. *Strategic Entrepreneurship Journal, 9*(1), 99-117.

Robins, S., & Mayer, R. E. (1993). Schema training in analogical reasoning. *Journal of Educational Psychology, 85*(3), 529.

Social Desirability Bias [SDB]: We want to be accepted by others, and are more likely to say or do things we don't actually believe to seek their approval.

Much of our knowledge about human thoughts and actions is self-reported. Yet, studies of what individuals claim and what they do show unique differences. A classic example involves opinion surveys on controversial topics: people with uncommon views are less likely to answer honestly out of fear of being rejected. Interestingly, even efforts to warn respondents can sometimes backfire.

In time management, this sometimes manifests as giving optimistic schedules to impress others or pessimistic estimates to communicate the complexity of work.

See also Bandwagon Effect [BWE], Groupthink [GT]

Clifford, S., & Jerit, J. (2015). Do attempts to improve respondent attention increase social desirability bias?. *Public Opinion Quarterly, 79*(3), 790-802.

Stodel, M. (2015). But what will people think?: Getting beyond social desirability bias by increasing cognitive load. *International Journal of Market Research, 57*(2), 313-322.

> **Sleep-enhanced learning [SEL]**: A short nap can increase your retention of information by up to a factor of five.

Extensive research into the relationship between sleep and brain function shows a variety of powerful effects. Unsurprisingly, sleep deprivation severely limits cognitive capacity, especially with regard to memory and problem-solving. Starting a task when fully rested also increases efficacy.

Interestingly, a brief nap immediately following a study session can dramatically improve how much you remember. Scientists believe that the restful state may strengthen neural pathways and facilitate later recall.

See also Dual Process Theory [DPT], Intentional Blindness Effect [IBE]

Genzel, L. (2018). *Investigating the effect of sleep on different spatial learning.* Unpublished manuscript.

Noack, H., Schick, W., Mallot, H., & Born, J. (2017). Sleep enhances knowledge of routes and regions in spatial environments. *Learning & Memory, 24*(3), 140-144.

> **Self-fulfilling Prophecy [SFP]**: When our expectations of ourselves or others tend to influence perspectives or actions, making what we anticipate a reality.

A broad concept that spans literature, sociology, business, and philosophy, outcomes are often determined in part by our predictions. For example if many people believe that a particular location is "cursed" than any retail operation that opens there is likely to fail. This is not because their products or services are faulty, but because the marketplace has pre-ordained their future.

In psychology, many phenomena are classified as self-fulfilling prophecies. Consider those cases in which a placebo is as effective as actual medicine. Another is the Pygmalion Effect, first demonstrated in the 1960s when teachers were told that a particular group of pupils were "gifted." The identified students outperformed their peers, but in truth they were selected at random. Because the teachers *believed* they were exceptional, they were given extra attention.

In workplaces, believing you can—or believing you can't—is often the greatest predictor of an outcome. Instead, actively focus on facts and data instead of what individuals believe about coworkers, customers, or competitors.

See also Emotional Contagion [EC], Hawthorne Effect [HWE]

Jussim, L. (1986). Self-fulfilling prophecies: A theoretical and integrative review. *Psychological Review, 93*(4), 429

Jussim, L., & Stevens, S. T. (2016). Why accuracy dominates self-fulfilling prophecies and bias. *Interpersonal and Intrapersonal Expectancies*, 110-116.

Sitting-induced Anxiety [SIA]: Being seated too long can cause us to become anxious.

Recent headlines in the popular press have claimed that "Sitting is the New Smoking." Although this may seem extreme, research indicates that we spend more time seated than in previous generations which leads to negative impacts on our physical and mental health.

In particular, sitting is associated with anxiety and other forms of stress. Individuals can promote mindful behavior by engaging in minor activities such as walking or stretching. When conducted briefly but frequently such interventions can wholly counteract the measurable negative impacts of prolonged sitting.

See also Mindfulness [MFL]

Milton, K., Gale, J., Stamatakis, E., & Bauman, A. (2015). Trends in prolonged sitting time among European adults: 27 country analysis. *Preventive Medicine, 77*, 11-16.

Teychenne, M., Costigan, S. A., & Parker, K. (2015). The association between sedentary behaviour and risk of anxiety: a systematic review. *BMC Public Health, 15*(1), 513.

Yang, C. H., & Conroy, D. E. (2018). Momentary negative affect is lower during mindful movement than while sitting: An experience sampling study. *Psychology of Sport and Exercise, 37*, 109-116.

Self-verification Theory [SVT]: We prefer that others see us as we see ourselves.

Individuals collect beliefs and values over the course of their lives. In contexts where others correctly identify these positions, we feel supported and confident. However, sharing our views involves a risk of rejection. We must navigate this friction in all our relationships.

Research into this concept shows a variety of benefits. Job candidates who self-verify have greater success, and individual contributors who do so improve workplace performance. Self-verification also increases behavioral predictability, which leads to trustworthiness and authenticity.

The competing approach, self-enhancement, emphasizes being praised over being genuine. While generally viewed as less effective for overall self-concept, self-enhancement can lead to short term gains in organizations.

See also Outcome vs. Process Orientation [OPO], Power Paradox [PP]

Ferris, D. L., Lian, H., Brown, D. J., & Morrison, R. (2015). Ostracism, self-esteem, and job performance: When do we self-verify and when do we self-enhance?. *Academy of Management Journal, 58*(1), 279-297.

Moore, C., Lee, S. Y., Kim, K., & Cable, D. M. (2017). The advantage of being oneself: The role of applicant self-verification in organizational hiring decisions. *Journal of Applied Psychology, 102*(11), 1493.

Zeigarnik Effect [ZE]: We remember incomplete or interrupted tasks better than those which we have finished.

Named for a Russian psychologist, this effect was first associated with waiters who seemed only able to remember what was ordered before the bill had been paid. Similarly, studies in which participants are interrupted during a warmup task show reduced efficacy on the primary task.

Evidence implies that when we can control interruptions—or if we can at least create a plan to finish incomplete work—we are more productive and less stressed.

See also Doorway Effect [DWE], Mindfulness [MFL]

Masicampo, E. J., & Baumeister, R. F. (2011). Consider it done! Plan making can eliminate the cognitive effects of unfulfilled goals. Journal of Personality and Social Psychology, 101(4), 667.

Kupor, D. M., Reich, T., & Shiv, B. (2015). Can't finish what you started? The effect of climactic interruption on behavior. Journal of Consumer Psychology, 25(1), 113-119.